Praise for *Finding Mrs. Warnecke*

"Thank goodness for Cindi, who shows us that teaching is both messy and magical. Through her stories—of students with overwhelming personal issues, dilapidated classrooms with limited supplies, and one young, resolved, idealistic teacher—she reveals that the key to successful teaching is loving our students and helping them develop dignity and self-respect . . .

"As I read this inspiring story, my mind went back to those memorable teachers who changed my life. Cindi not only makes us believe in the power of teaching to change lives, she reminds us that changing lives is what teaching is all about. I came away from this book with a full heart—ready to teach tomorrow and for many tomorrows to come."

—from the foreword by Donalyn Miller, 6th grade language arts teacher and best-selling author of *The Book Whisperer*

"This book substantiates the *power* of great teachers to change young lives. That would be enough, but it also reveals the *secret* of great teachers, that they see themselves and their classrooms through the eyes of their students."

—James Cunningham, Ph.D., professor emeritus, University of North Carolina at Chapel Hill and co-author of *What Really Matters in Writing*

"Every journey of discovery begins with a belief that something or someone is worth finding. In *Finding Mrs. Warnecke,* Cindi Rigsbee has written a book worth finding. The book is much more than a nostalgic search for a childhood teacher, it is about the value of seeking something that has been lost within us all."

—Anthony J. Mullen, 2009 National Teacher of the Year

"I cry every time I read Cindi's words or hear her story . . . it takes me back to Mrs. Perry, who is the reason I became a science teacher, and why I am where I am today. *Finding Mrs. Warnecke* tells of a great emotional and professional journey—it is a book that no quality educator will dare miss."

—Elic Senter, North Carolina Teaching Fellow, consultant with the North Carolina Association of Educators, and mayor of Franklinton, North Carolina

finding Mrs. Warnecke

THE DIFFERENCE TEACHERS MAKE

Cindi Rigsbee

FOREWORD BY DONALYN MILLER

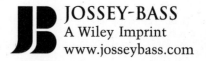

JOSSEY-BASS
A Wiley Imprint
www.josseybass.com

Published by Jossey-Bass
A Wiley Imprint
989 Market Street, San Francisco, CA 94103-1741—www.josseybass.com

Jossey-Bass books and products are available through most bookstores. To contact Jossey-Bass directly call our Customer Care Department within the U.S. at 800-956-7739, outside the U.S. at 317-572-3986, or fax 317-572-4002.

Jossey-Bass also publishes its books in a variety of electronic formats. Some content that appears in print may not be available in electronic books.

Library of Congress Cataloging-in-Publication Data
Rigsbee, Cindi, 1959–
    Finding Mrs. Warnecke : the difference teachers make/Cindi Rigsbee.
        p. cm.
    ISBN 978-0-470-48678-8 (cloth)
    1. Teachers—Conduct of life. 2. Motivation in education.
    3. Student-centered learning. I. Title.
    LB1775.R524 2010
    371.1—dc22

                                                    2009047061

Printed in the United States of America
FIRST EDITION

HB Printing 10 9 8 7 6 5 4 3 2 1

CONTENTS

ABOUT THE AUTHOR

*To Barbara Warnecke, who helped me find myself
at six and then again at fifty. My sincere
thanks go out to "Mrs. Teacher."*

Cindi **Rigsbee** is a National Board Certified Teacher™ with more than twenty years of experience in the classroom. She has taught high school English and drama, as well as middle school language arts, dance, drama, and reading. Rigsbee has been named Teacher of the Year at the schoolwide, districtwide, and statewide levels, and in 2009 she was one of four finalists for National Teacher of the Year. In September 2008, she appeared on *Good Morning America* to explain the life-changing impact her first-grade teacher, Barbara Warnecke, had on her. A frequent contributor to *Teacher Magazine* online, Rigsbee also publishes a blog called The Dream Teacher (www.thedreamteacher .blogspot.com).

ACKNOWLEDGMENTS

There's a reason authors include an acknowledgments page: no one writes a book alone. There are so many people who've influenced my path as a teacher and now as a writer that the list may be longer than the book itself. But I'll give it a try.

First, I sincerely thank the school administrators who gave me a chance at teaching, who didn't give up on me when I wasn't very good at it, and who encouraged me by helping me grow professionally along the way—thank you Edison Watson, Wayne Adcock, Winston Kerley, Danny Thomas, Raymond Paris, Calvin Dobbins, Juanita Jones, Ada Setzer, Barbara Hastings, Rich Kozak, and my current bosses, Jason Johnson, Tiffany Stuart, and Greg Hicks, who have taught me so much about how to teach.

The list of teachers who inspired me, worked in the trenches beside me, and taught me something about myself as an educator is lengthy, but here goes . . . Lynn Church, Fred Westbrook, Beth Strecker, Marian Salyer, Kim Strickland, Shirley Mull, Jean Ransom, Eric Collins, Carla Kirkland, Grayling Williams, Alissa Griffith, Kelly Scearce, Michele Nease, Judson Parrish, Alice Hagaman, Vicki Buckner, and especially my BFFs—Heather Walton, Cristie Watson,

Jenny Freudenberg, Kelly Kaplan, and Amy Richardson—you all had a part in making me the teacher I am. Thank you.

To Orange County Schools and the faculty and staff of Gravelly Hill Middle School, thank you for being there with me as we work so hard for the children of Orange County. I have never worked with a group of individuals so committed to excellence, and you make me better every day that I have the honor of standing side by side with you.

I have been so lucky to have been named the North Carolina Teacher of the Year and as a result able to work with phenomenal educators who have raised the bar for me when I think of what a teacher is. Thank you to the wonderful individuals I've had the chance to work with because of the Teacher of the Year program: Dan Holloman, Paige Elliott, Trisha Muse, Bernard Waugh, RuthAnn Parker, Sonya Rinehart, Freida Baker, Renee Peoples, Janice Raper, Carolyn Sneeden, Diana Beasley, Vicki Rivenbark, Ginger Holloway, Monty Coggins, Mike Shaw, Wanda Fernandez, Catherine Allen, and the 2009 State Teachers of the Year, who are my kindred spirits all over the country.

To Barnett Berry, Ann Byrd, Alice Williams, and the staff at the Center for Teaching Quality, thank you for allowing me to participate in the Teacher Leaders Network, the teacher's lounge in heaven. I have learned more from you and some of the most brilliant teachers in the country during the past two years than from any other professional development opportunity I've ever had.

To those who undergirded my passion as a writer—to John Norton, my editor on the mountain, your belief in my writing gave me the confidence to put those *Teacher Magazine* articles out there. Without those, I wouldn't be here. I am forever grateful. To Holly Holland, thank you for helping me understand how this process works. You patiently frontloaded me with information that has been invaluable. And to my editors at Jossey-Bass, Marjorie McAneny and Leslie Tilley, you believed in a complete stranger, took thoughts on paper, and made me an author. I am moved beyond words about this experience.

To my "best friends I never see"—to Lula Osborn and Evalee Parker, it sounds cliché, but thank you for always being there. Lu-ler, no matter how far apart we are, you always manage to keep us close. You've stuck by me for twenty years, and that has given me great comfort. Evalee, when I told you that my book proposal would be rejected by twenty-five publishers, you said, "Then send twenty-six!" Thank you for not giving up, even when I almost did.

To my family—to my husband, David, who has been more excited than anyone throughout this process—I would have starved without you. Thank you for supporting me unconditionally. To my children, Heather, Kelli, Erin, and Will, you have given me inspiration for writing all along the way and have been my in-house "students" at times when you probably wished that your mom-stepmom had been anything but a teacher. Thank you for indulging me and letting me be a little crazy. Sometimes crazy equals creative, and you all encouraged that. To my grandchildren, Reaghan, Cannon, Taylor, Piper, and Baylee, you are always the best diversion there is for a stressed-out writer. Thank you for adding a joy to my life that I could never have imagined. To my brother and sister, Jim and Lisa, you shared the life that I tried so hard to depict accurately. Jim, I only hope I have half the writing talent that you do. Lisa, you and I have held each other up for fifty years. I wish for fifty more. Mama, you were my first teacher, and you never gave up on me even when I messed up in my life, which was often. I have been blessed to have a mother like you. And to my Daddy, I'm painfully sorry that you weren't here to witness this amazing event in my life. Your spirit was with me in every word I wrote. I know that you have now found peace.

To Mrs. Warnecke—of course there would be no book without you. I am thankful to Brian O'Keefe and the folks at *Good Morning America* for finding you after forty-five years and am glad we're spending our remaining time making up for those years we missed. Thank you for having a no-holds-barred attitude about this book, saying "Use anything . . . quotes, descriptions, memories. There are no limits." There are no limits to my thanks to you.

And, last, to the more than two thousand North Carolina students who, despite tremendous hardships, have made an effort to sit in school desks and listen to me for the past thirty years—I have been energized by your energy and able to love because of the love that I've felt from you. In years to come, when I look at this book, I'll see your faces looking back at me. I'm proud that I had the opportunity to know you, and I hope I made a difference in your lives.

FOREWORD
by Donalyn Miller

indi Rigsbee's reputation precedes her—North Carolina Teacher of the Year, National Teacher of the Year finalist, with 20-plus years in the classroom—a knowledgeable and talented member of the teaching profession. I met Cindi through our work in the Teacher Leadership Network. Reading her impassioned posts about working with students, I've been inspired by her practical approach to teaching.

Her passion, her common sense, her experience, her love for students—Cindi expertly weaves these threads into a magical story in this compelling book. Her teaching expertise has evolved through years of trial and error, but she believes the lessons she learned almost a half century ago, in the first-grade classroom of Barbara Warnecke, first showed her the secrets of masterful teaching. After a rocky start in first grade, stuck in a crowded classroom with a teacher who seemed to dislike children, Cindi and a few classmates were reassigned to a new teacher's class, in a makeshift basement room with caterpillars climbing the walls. Little did Cindi know this would become one of her favorite places on Earth.

Mrs. Warnecke created a loving, exciting learning environment, where each child felt special. She planted the early seeds of Cindi's love for reading and writing, encouraging her to write poetry and giving her books to read. Mrs. Warnecke believed in her kids—she showed them through her words and actions that she knew they were capable of greatness, and cheered them on. Once Cindi became a teacher herself, these lessons of love and acceptance from Mrs. Warnecke started shaping her teaching path. She recalls, "I began to understand that accepting all my students, regardless of the misfortunes they dealt with on a daily basis, would be the key to being able to teach them."

I've read many books by "super teachers," those who seem to magically know how to lead a class, design instruction, and motivate kids. Teaching, for me, has always been messier. I could never produce the same magical results those gurus do, often feeling inferior and questioning my abilities.

Thank goodness for Cindi, who shows us that teaching is both messy and magical. Through her stories—of students with overwhelming personal issues, dilapidated classrooms with limited supplies, and one young, resolved, idealistic teacher—she reveals that the key to successful teaching is loving our students and helping them develop dignity and self-respect. Cindi believes each of us has a Mrs. Warnecke, a teacher who made a difference in our lives, and she urges us to become "Mrs. Warneckes" for our students. We *can* make a difference; we can impact kids' lives in ways we may never realize.

Barbara Warnecke changed little Cindy Cole's life in first grade, and in turn, influenced the lives of Cindi Rigsbee's students. As I read this inspiring story, my mind went back to those memorable teachers who changed my life. Cindi not only makes us believe in the power of teaching to change lives, she reminds us that changing lives is what teaching is all about. I came away from this book with a full heart—ready to teach tomorrow and for many tomorrows to come.

PROLOGUE

I t's January 2009. I'm sitting in the seat assigned to the Teacher Adviser for the North Carolina State Board of Education. It's an important place to be, a role I take very seriously, and I feel it every time I'm here. Sometimes there are news cameras around, and I wonder if the folks at home in their dens will see me and wonder what in heaven's name a teacher from rural Orange County, North Carolina, has done to deserve this honor. I scan across the rows of observers in the room, an audience of important people on the education scene in my state—staff at the Department of Public Instruction, representatives from various educational professional organizations, and guests who appear to be in awe of the process here. I look around at the members of the board, a group that genuinely holds our children's best interests at heart, people who truly have their fingers on the pulse of the classrooms in our state. This is a room where education policy is discussed and passed with a hearty "Motion carries!" I always find myself shocked to be a part of it.

More than once in the six months I have served as the Teacher Adviser to the board, I've asked myself "Why me?" I know I'm here by virtue of the fact that I've had the honor of serving as the North Carolina Teacher of the Year for the past few months, but that's yet another reason I continually ask "Why *me*?" I often think about the thousands of deserving teachers in my state, and I wonder, as usual, if I'm representing them well. My thoughts are interrupted as the chairman of the board calls for a five-minute break.

I notice the state superintendent, Dr. June Atkinson, waving to me from her seat at the head of the board table. She motions me over and points toward the hallway. By the time I join her, in a corner of the hall just beside the elevators, she is grinning at me. I can't imagine what she's about to say.

Then she takes my hands, and we stand face-to-face, like two little schoolgirls on the playground. "Cindi," she says, "I've gotten a call from the Council of Chief State School Officers. You have been chosen as one of four finalists for the National Teacher of the Year!" I feel the color leave my face, and I silently beg my knees not to buckle. The only words I can muster are words of disbelief, compelling phrases like "You're kidding" and "Are you sure?" Before she can answer, Dr. Atkinson is called away momentarily, and I'm left alone to absorb the shocking, yet exciting, news.

My head is swimming as I return to my seat, and I try to remain focused for the duration of the meeting. I've thought many times, while carrying out my Teacher of the Year role, that I won't get away with this for long . . . that the world will eventually find out about my rough start as a teacher. When I speak to teacher groups, I say, "I struggled as a beginning teacher." I'm not sure "struggled" is the right word. Maybe I downright *stunk*. Maybe I just didn't know what to do, or I didn't have the amount of support I needed. In any case, as I sit here, I understand my fear—that someone, a former student or colleague, is going to appear and say, "I was there during her first year teaching. It wasn't pretty. She certainly doesn't deserve to be her state's Teacher of the Year."

I'm aware of one thing: I'd better find some confidence to pull off this next role—that of National Teacher of the Year finalist— or I will be, as my students say, "stone-cold busted." Right there during the break, I do some brainstorming. I ask myself the following questions: Why have these honors come my way? How did I get from "Below Standard" on my teacher evaluations to a finalist for National Teacher of the Year?

I begin to make a list, an answer to my own questions, on the back of a handout, and unsurprisingly, the first thing I write is the word "relationships." I know that anything positive I've ever done as a teacher can be related back to that one word. The relationships I foster with my students get me out of bed and on the interstate headed to my school every day. There was a time when I didn't understand the importance of making connections with the children in my care. Now it's difficult for me to remember a time like that.

The next word I write is "magic." One thing I think that has made me a better teacher is the effort I put into making my classroom a magical place. I know that it's my goal for students to *want* to learn from me, and taking four walls, a white board, and some student desks and making them warm and inviting enables me to meet that goal. Fostering an atmosphere of family is important to me, and finding the "magical" elements that make my classroom a place my students want to be is one of my most important goals.

Next, I think of my classroom back home, and see the words *Whatever It Takes* above my board in front of the room. My commitment to do whatever I have to do to make my classroom a safe and happy place for learning is one reason that I have been able to put those struggling years behind me and make a difference as a teacher. I realize that there are times when the job is tough and the hours are long, but I will do whatever it takes to make a difference in the lives of my students.

The last word I add to my list is "dreams." I don't even need to add any narrative to my makeshift notes. I know what this one means, having been called the "Dream Teacher" by my students for almost fifteen years now. I believe in dreams, and I believe in going after them with passion and perseverance. I share that passion with my students on the first day of school and throughout the year. And I encourage them to pursue their own dreams and passions.

So now I sit here, mind reeling, and stare at those words scribbled on scrap paper. *Maybe there are some reasons that I've turned out OK as a teacher; maybe I've almost figured it out,* I say to myself.

And then, even louder, my thoughts continue: *I know what I need to do about the news I've just received.*

I need to call Mrs. Warnecke . . .

finding
Mrs. Warnecke

❧ "There was a connection back there."

—B. WARNECKE, SEPTEMBER 5, 2008

ONE

Looking for Stars

My brother was already in school by the time I was born, and my earliest memory is of Jimmy going to school every day, leaving me to think of the future when I could go to "big school" myself. In the afternoons I would press my nose against the picture window in the den, watching for the big yellow school bus and listening for the screech of air brakes as the bus stopped at the top of the hill to deliver Jimmy home.

Finally, in August 1963, the time came for me to start school. I felt so grown up when my mother took me to Pic 'n Pay to buy school shoes. Back then girls were required to wear dresses, and to go with them, Mama purchased saddle oxfords that I hated and shiny black patent leather shoes that I loved. I called them Sunday School shoes. For years, whenever I would hear the clip-clop of shoes on hardwood, I would think *Sunday School shoes*. My mother, a talented seamstress, made many of my dresses for me. She could do amazing things with rickrack and smocking. Plaid jumpers and skirts were the style of the first grade that year, and Mama made sure I went to school with the best-pressed version she could afford.

At the time, in Durham, North Carolina, where I grew up, there was no public kindergarten, so my first year of school was first grade. My birthday is in September, so I was usually the youngest in my class, and often began the school year feeling behind. But first grade was different. I didn't know I was the youngest; I was just giddy with excitement. I'd never been a quiet child at home, and I'm sure my parents were just as ready for me to be in school as I was to go—surely some of my energy would be consumed there.

There was one problem that kept me from being a carefree little first grader: the teacher hated me.

When I arrived at Bragtown Elementary, though, my heart was broken. School was nothing like what I had hoped it would be, even though we were learning to read, something all first graders look forward to doing. I was placed in the redbird group, and even as a five-year-old I knew that the redbirds could read better than the bluebirds or the blackbirds. But there was one problem that kept me from being a carefree little first grader: the teacher hated me.

Mrs. Riley looked to me as if she was at least ninety years old, with a lopsided bun atop her head and menacing granny glasses perched on her nose. I don't remember her ever smiling unless she was talking to one particular student: Sheila.

Sheila was beautiful, a blue-eyed, blonde-haired cherub. She looked like a doll, and everyone in class worked hard to befriend her. I remember the day she told me where she lived—"It's right behind the candy store," she said. Then I knew she really *was* enchanted.

My mother and Sheila's mother were the grade mother chairs—they worked together to arrange all the class parties and to ensure that cupcakes were brought to every school event. When they met to plan, I got to visit Sheila's house behind the candy store. It was a wonderland of toys, including Barbie and all her accessories. Sheila had a section of the den reserved just for her Barbie stuff—the Barbie house, the Barbie Corvette, the Barbie pool . . . all things Barbie.

At home, I pulled leaves off of trees, stirred them in a pot to play house, and dressed up my cat (who was much less accommodating than Barbie). My sister and I played in the lot behind our house, a dumping ground for old pipes, pieces of concrete, and slabs of wood. We literally yelled out to Mama, "We're going to play in the junkyard" as we ran off to our version of a playground. So the world Sheila lived in was a different one, and I knew it right away—but felt no envy, as small children are innocent about such things. She was my friend, and I loved her.

Mrs. Riley adored her too, and didn't try to hide that fact from the rest of the class. When it became obvious that the teacher had an errand to be run, I would slide to the edge of my desk and raise my hand as high as I could. But it was always Sheila who went and Sheila who collected the ice cream and milk money and distributed the ice cream and milk. Later on, in fifth grade, she would be the beautiful witch Glinda in the Bragtown School production of *The Wizard of Oz*.

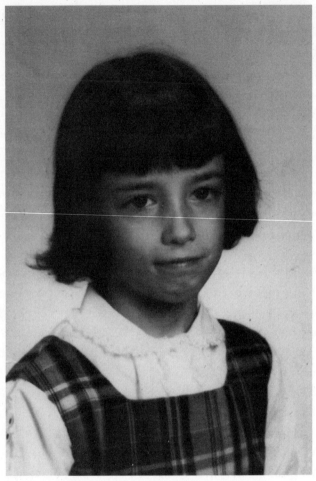

In first grade I could barely muster a smile.

With my brown eyes and unruly black hair, I was the Wicked Witch of the West to Sheila's Glinda. And I was skinny—no matter how much I ate, my weight never seemed to catch up to my height. I was sure that if I were prettier or blonder, or had a houseful of

Barbies, Mrs. Riley would like me more. But the more I tried to please her, the more annoyed she seemed. I can remember her impatience as we read. A mispronounced word could easily bring a frown or a grimace. (Of course, I wasn't the only one on the receiving end of these looks; my friend in the bluebird group finally refused to read, too intimidated by Mrs. Riley's fearsome expressions.) First grade was proving to be a grave disappointment for an eager student.

Down to the Basement, out of the Darkness

A month into the school year, the principal came to the classroom door and told us that our class had too many students. I immediately grew excited about first grade all over again at the thought of a new teacher. The principal proceeded to divide us into two classes. When he called my name, I was thrilled at being selected to move to a new room.

Later, as a teacher, I realized that the selection process most likely consisted of old Mrs. Riley looking at her class roster and murmuring *I don't want her, I don't want him, I don't want her . . .* as she

I realized that the selection process most likely consisted of old Mrs. Riley looking at her class roster and murmuring I don't want her, I don't want him, I don't want her . . . *as she checked our names off her list. But it turns out that rejection can be a positive thing.*

checked our names off her list. But it turns out that rejection can be a positive thing. What would happen in the next few months would affect my confidence and self-esteem, and eventually my career choice and teaching philosophy. And all of that can be attributed to one person: a twenty-three-year-old teacher named Barbara Warnecke.

I remember it like this: the principal lined us up in Mrs. Riley's classroom and led us down the hall, clip-clopping in our hard-soled shoes on wooden floors with forty years' worth of wax on them, and out the back door—the door that led to the gymnasium. The only time I had ever been in the musty, high-ceilinged gym, I'd learned the hokey pokey and I shook it all about. I remember how dusty it was in there—I could hardly breathe—and I was horrified at the thought that our new class might be held in there. So I was relieved when the principal turned left at the gym door and continued on down the concrete path. But then he abruptly turned left again, which made no sense. There was no classroom there— just the basement at the bottom of some stairs.

We had never given that damp place a thought as we ran by it on the way to the playground, but down the stairs the principal went, and we followed right behind him, like little ducklings. At the bottom was a room that in many ways did look like a classroom. There were clunky wooden desks and a black chalkboard. But behind a closet door that someone jerked open were beady little eyes that stared back at us. John, the cutest boy in the first grade, grinned and told us that those eyes belonged to rats, and for the rest of the year the biggest boys in the classroom would torment the rest of us by threatening to open that door. All of us, bullies and victims alike, hung our coats on hooks on the back wall that year.

Then we sat in those big desks and waited. I traced my finger over initials that some former student had carved long ago. For a moment I thought we would soon be escorted back upstairs, back to Mrs. Riley and Sheila. But then in walked Mrs. Warnecke, a pretty young teacher with a teased bob hairstyle and a smile that filled the entire classroom. She looked happy to be with us—with *me*—and she didn't even seem too scared of the closet. The principal

My Mrs. Teacher.

introduced her, pronouncing her name with care (WAR-nek-ee), but we still couldn't say it. For months she would be "Mrs. Teacher." She passed out *Dick and Jane* books, and we got right to work.

I remember being distracted that first day in Mrs. Warnecke's class. I kept wondering how we would get to the bathroom in time. Our classroom was *outside,* for goodness' sake. We were first graders! The next day I decided to research the issue. I asked Mrs. Teacher if I could "be excused," just the way my Mama had taught me. I walked up the basement steps, around between the gym and the back of the first-grade hall, up the stairs and into the building. The minute I opened the door to the hallway, I regretted it. I saw a sixth-grade boy coming toward me, and I was embarrassed—of all days for me to be wearing those clumsy saddle oxfords! I hung my head and tried to slip past him, but he stopped right in front of me.

"What's your name?" he asked.

"Cindy," I answered, not looking up.

"I like those shoes," he said as he walked around me to continue down the hall.

I skipped on to the bathroom and then back to the basement, and that was the end of my concern about the number of steps to the bathroom—and about my shoes. I still hung my head at the sight of sixth-grade boys, though.

More Discoveries

Not all of my problems were solved by my new teacher, of course. I wrestled with my self-confidence, which my mother attributes to my little sister, Lisa, coming along when I was only fourteen months old. Mama remembers me in the grocery store, just barely walking, standing to the side and looking confused as shoppers stopped to admire the new baby and totally ignored me. But even though I may have been sad at the sudden shift in everyone's attention, I adored my sister as soon as she was born.

I was glad not to have to share my first-grade class with her, though. School was mine that year, and everything that happened in there was my own magical world. *School was mine that year, and everything that happened in there was my own magical world.* I had a loving teacher who turned a dark classroom into a warm place to be, and the experience was finally turning out to be everything I had wished for.

One day Mrs. Warnecke surprised us during ice cream time. Every day we would bring our ice cream money and then tell Mrs. Teacher which kind we wanted—ice cream sandwich, fudgesicle, or vanilla cup. One afternoon after we turned in our money and placed our usual orders, Mrs. Warnecke said, "I have a surprise for you. I didn't get your regular ice cream today." Instead she pulled out vanilla popsicles covered with a hard chocolate coating. This may not sound like much, but to a room full of first graders, it was like Christmas morning! We squealed and bit into the hard coating while commenting on each bite. For years I thought she had planned the whole thing. I really believed that those same popsicles had been available all year, and that she had withheld them from us so that we could be surprised later. Of course, most likely that particular type of ice cream became available only that very day. But that ice cream adventure made us feel special and loved.

And that was the disposition of our classroom during that entire year.

When caterpillars would climb on the damp basement walls, Mrs. Teacher would merely pluck them off and talk to us about them—seizing the opportunity to have a science lesson whenever the opportunity presented itself. I remember that we had to rest on blue and red mats daily after lunch. I was somewhat anxious at the thought of lying on that basement floor; I had visions of all kinds of critters crawling on me when I was asleep. But every day Mrs. Warnecke would direct us to our mats, then walk around and gently touch each of us on the shoulder, one at a time. We were a quilt of six-year-olds on that wooden floor, all calmed and soothed by the caring demeanor of our new teacher.

Mrs. Warnecke plays with us on the Bragtown School playground.

Science was OK, but my love was reading. I loved words even then. Being able to look at a book and know it said "See Puff run" was amazing to me. So once I was able to write words myself, on inch-high lines with a fat first-grade pencil, I tried my hand at my first poem. It was titled "Stars."

> *Stars, stars*
> *I'll find out where they are.*
> *They shine at night*
> *Til morning bright.*
> *No one can tell*
> *Where they have fell.*
> *Stars, stars.*

In time I would grow up to be an English major and learn the job of a past participle, but in first grade I just wanted to rhyme. I shyly took my creation up to Mrs. Warnecke's desk and looked down at the scratched wooden basement floor while she read. When she was finished, she grabbed me, hugged me, and said, "This is beautiful. I want you to write many, many more of these."

I took her at her word. I continued to write little poems every year. In second grade I wrote a little ditty about the seasons. And then I trotted my skinny second-grade legs down to Mrs. Warnecke's room so that she could read it. And even though she had another class by then, a roomful of children she had to teach, whenever I would visit her, she treated me as if I were the only child in the room. I hope that the poem I wrote about teachers was a partial repayment:

Teachers are quite nice, I think
but that is only me.
Other people just don't know
How nice a teacher can be.

A few years later, our school newspaper, the *Bragtown Bugle,* accepted a couple of my poems for publication. I was proud, my mother was proud, and Mrs. Warnecke was proud. But my pride was mixed with sadness—Mrs. Warnecke was moving away. She gave me a gift when she left. It was, of course, a book of poems: *You Read to Me, I'll Read to You,* by John Ciardi. She inscribed it "May each of us think of the other whenever a poem is read. Barbara Warnecke, June, 1967."

Mrs. Parrish

What makes a shy young girl decide at the ripe old age of ten that she wants to be a teacher? Only the inspiration of a great teacher would guide a student to make this life-changing decision.

My life was influenced by my fifth-grade teacher at Wiley Elementary School in Salisbury, NC. Mrs. Ollie Mae Parrish, a petite red-haired lady who commanded respect from her students, was the teacher who changed my life. By the end of the fifth grade, I knew that I wanted to be a teacher just like Mrs. Parrish.

Elementary school was quite different during my days. We were well behaved; we sat in rows and spoke only when we were allowed. We walked in straight lines down the hall.

Girls wore dresses to school, and we carried metal lunch boxes. But Mrs. Parrish was the teacher who allowed us to be individuals in her room. She talked about her husband, Harry, like he was our friend. She stood up for us when the PE teacher was mean to our class. She was angry when we had to go to school on a Saturday to make up a snow day; she made that day fun! Mrs. Parrish was that teacher who actually talked to her students.

My most vivid memory from Mrs. Parrish's class was our study of the United States. She divided us into groups, something unheard of during those days, and gave us a section of the country to study. We had to create a bulletin board section of the classroom that represented our region and share what we learned with the class. *We* were the teachers! No one in my elementary career had ever allowed me to create a lesson for my class. Mrs. Parrish was ahead of her time.

Mrs. Parrish took this very shy girl, smaller and younger than the others, and made me a stronger student. I was too nervous to read aloud, but she saw an opportunity to give me courage to stand in front of others and share what I had learned.

I never forgot Mrs. Parrish as I continued to work to become a teacher. While I was in college, I visited her classroom to observe her magic at work. I also worked hard to keep in touch with her as I started my teaching career.

My shining moment with Mrs. Parrish came quite a few years later. Some of my students were presenting their projects to parents and friends on the latest technology using our new Apple computers. It was an evening performance, and the room was full. As I stood to introduce my students and share background information on what we had done, I saw a smiling face that was very familiar to me. In the audience was Mrs. Parrish—so proud of that shy little fifth grader she had taught so many years before.

Mrs. Parrish is teaching in heaven now, and I am sure she has it quite organized! I am currently in my thirty-third year of teaching in North Carolina. My one wish in my life as a teacher is that I will one day have a student say that I made a lasting influence on his or her life.

—Janice Raper, Academically/Intellectually Gifted teacher, Hurley Elementary School, Salisbury, North Carolina, 2008–2009 North Carolina Northwest Regional Teacher of the Year

Years of Change

So, four years after rescuing me, Mrs. Warnecke and her husband, who had just graduated from Duke University, returned to their home in Buffalo, New York. To a child, it seemed a world away, but it was OK.

By then I was ten years old. Soon I would enter junior high and grapple with the distractions of those tumultuous teen years. And there were other distractions in the South in the late 1960s. Bragtown School was an all-white elementary school until desegregation was mandated in 1969. My neighborhood was an inner-city mixture of black and white. So all through my elementary years, I got on my bus and rode to Bragtown while my black neighbors headed to their bus stops to be taken to Lakeview Elementary.

The next year, as a seventh grader, I attended school with black students for the first time. Three girls approached me in the bathroom on the first day of school and asked me how it felt to be white. One day a white boy stood in the front of my school bus, just as it stopped to let him off. He drew attention to himself by singing a few lines of "Dixie," then jumped out the door. Ten black boys jumped from seats all around me and chased after him down the street.

As alarming as that incident was, I think I was most nervous about the need for police escorts to and from school. White adults protesting desegregation lined the streets from my neighborhood to my school and threw rocks at the buses. The happy memories of my elementary years sometimes dimmed in those difficult days.

But still I felt special when I got home from school to see that Mrs. Warnecke had sent me a letter. I received the last one in 1970, when I was thirteen. By then I was sporting a mouth full of metal braces and had changed the spelling of my name to Cindi, with an *i* at the end. There were three other Cindys in my classes, and I wanted to be unique and interesting . . . interesting enough to be invited to the Cougar Club party, a Christmas ball attended by my school's student athletes and their dates. I was never asked to go.

I became a cheerleader, and adopted a corresponding personality that was useful for obscuring my continuing low self-esteem. My looks were, as always, the big issue for me, but other factors played a part. I was constantly aware that I was growing up in modest surroundings, that in the circles of the "haves" and the "have nots" my family would be considered "having just enough." We weren't hungry by any means, but there were few extras like family vacations, color televisions, and nice cars. My grandmother didn't have a functioning bathroom in her house until after I was grown and married. (I do believe that Granny's outhouse was character building, though.)

Like most adolescents, I felt my way through my teen years. And though I gradually thought less and less about Mrs. Warnecke, her spirit was in me. I kept the book she had given me long after other childhood books had been discarded, and from time to time I would leaf through it. Still, it would be years before I would seriously think about seeing her again.

After high school, I headed to college with the love of literacy Mrs. Warnecke had nurtured in me years before. I remember thinking at some point in my junior year, around the time I declared my major in education, that I would like Mrs. Warnecke to know that I had made the decision to become a teacher. I don't think I was aware then of the impact she had made on my choice of a career, and I could not have known how her teaching practices would affect me as a teacher. But, at some level, I just wanted her to *know* that I would be following her path. At the time, though, it seemed impossible. We had lost touch, and the Internet would not come about for twenty years. So I continued to think fondly of my teacher from the elementary school basement, never dreaming that I would see her again someday.

Just as the words and the poetry that I came to love under Mrs. Warnecke's direction became a constant in my life, the unconditional affection and affirmation she had given me—without regard for my looks or lack of social status—molded and shaped me as a teacher. I would teach for twenty years before I fully understood her effect on me. And once I realized it, I hoped that someday she would know, if only I could find her. But finding her would be like that first poem; it would be like finding stars.

✽ "I felt very lost and unprepared."
—B. WARNECKE, NOVEMBER 12, 2008

TWO

Finding My Way

When I was growing up, it never occurred to me that I would some-day become a teacher. While my sister lined up her dolls in front of her pretend chalkboard to play "Miss Kilpatrick," a game she had named after *her* beloved first-grade teacher, I stayed outside for hours—jumping, flipping, and kicking. No, I didn't want to be a teacher. I wanted to be a Dallas Cowboys cheerleader.

I remember the day, back in junior high, when I saw our school's cheerleaders for the first time. They came bouncing into our school gymnasium, orange-and-white pleated skirts and orange pom-poms bright against the wooden bleachers, and I knew at that moment that I wanted to be on those sidelines with them: pleat-to-pleat with the popular girls. I pushed aside my lack of confidence and worked really hard during tryouts in seventh and eighth grade, but I was rejected both times. I watched as the prettier girls, many of whom just happened to be in the coach's homeroom, were chosen, Sheila among them.

During the ride home after the squads were named, I wept, heartbroken from the rejection. My mother soothed me, explaining that I could be anything I wanted to be if I worked hard enough. She encouraged me not to give up on my dream. So I worked.

My daddy had built a toolshed in the backyard, with a large window in the back of it made up of twenty panes surrounded by chipped white paint. I practiced tirelessly, using the windows as a mirror. Every night, I was out there jumping in front of that shed until past dark. I saved pennies and nickels in a shoebox marked "Money for Dance Lessons" and finally convinced my mother to scrape up the $12 a month it would take to finance gymnastics classes. When it came time for high school tryouts, I was at last selected for the team. This time, I cried again, laughing and sobbing simultaneously all the way home. By my senior year in high school, I was captain of the varsity cheerleading squad, and I placed second out of 350 campers at East Coast Cheerleading Camp for the honor of Most Outstanding Cheerleader. Through those experiences, I developed a newfound confidence. Although I continued to quietly wrestle with some of the same self-esteem issues that I had had in elementary school, I was all smiles when I put on my pleated skirt and my cheerleading shoes: saddle oxfords!

When I tried out for my college's cheerleading squad, however, I realized that sometimes dreams don't come true. I was one of two hundred young ladies who walked into the gym on my college campus for tryouts early in my freshman year. Although I was nervous, I made the first cut, to one hundred, and the next, to fifty, and the next, to twelve. Of those twelve, six would be chosen.

On the night of the announcement, I was number seven. In a cruel twist for a girl who had spent her entire life being teased for being too skinny, I was told that I weighed too much. How could this be? College cheers, it turns out, were different from those in high school. Most included stunts in which boys, some of whom weren't much bigger than I was, were supposed to lift me over their heads. I wasn't petite enough.

I was devastated. Going back to my dorm, I felt as if I were crawling along the sidewalk. I had spent all my high school years as a cheerleader and most of my spare time practicing. What would I do with myself? More important, who *was* I now?

Miss Clark

The day I saw public speaking on my class schedule was the day I told my mother, "I am dropping out of high school," even though we both knew it was just false bravado. Being a teacher was a goal I had fostered since the first grade when I erased all of my worksheets and played school with my younger brother. So fearfully, I returned to school the next day to embark on my speech class journey. Enter a teacher who terrified me, but eventually became one of the most influential people of my life, Miss Clark. She was loud, enthusiastic, had very high expectations, and frankly brought out a strong sense of awe from most of her students. At that time in my life, I fervently believed that Miss Clark was the embodiment of evil. For our first speech assignment she assigned an eight-page research paper along with an eight- to ten-minute informative speech. One of the parameters of the speech that I will never forget was that the delivery was to be primarily from memory, but we could use one note card. One note card! It took me about five or six tries, but I copied my entire research paper on that note card. Small fine print that went every which way; if that woman was going to force me to speak I was not going to forget what I had to say. When I presented that speech, I gave the whole eight-page research paper in three minutes flat, but I lived and did not fall flat on my face. I survived the speech and the class with some very insightful tricks given to me by Miss Clark. She did not allow me to revert back into my shyness, but kept giving me opportunities to discover my inner actress.

—Alice King, English/speech 10–12, Campbell County High School, Gillette, Wyoming, 2009 Wyoming Teacher of the Year

Changing My Dream

That night I took stock of my life, thinking about what I could do and what I cared about. I realized that I loved only one thing as much as cheerleading—my English class. I loved words, the magic of our language . . . poetry, essays, stories, plays. And it became clear that the love of literature had been a theme in my life, a thread that ran through all of my schooling, beginning with Mrs. Warnecke's first-grade class and the poetry we'd shared. I wanted to do *that*—to share that love, to quote Shakespeare to wide-eyed students who would be fascinated by the fact that "wherefore" means "why" and not "where." Then and there I became determined to follow the path of my favorite teacher and inspire others as Mrs. Warnecke had me.

Up until that point I hadn't even considered what my college major would be—I'd moved into my dorm that fall with visions of cheering at football games. But this sudden epiphany seemed so obvious: how could I not have thought of it before? Of course: I would teach! I began to picture my own classroom, and there I was, leading children to love school as I had as a first grader. I would be someone else's Mrs. Warnecke! The thought thrilled me.

I spent the next four years preparing to change the world, while writing practice lessons and studying educational theory. Although I sometimes felt a pang of sadness when I attended college ball games and watched the cheerleaders on the sidelines, I knew that my life held a deeper purpose. Some say teachers are "called" to the classroom. I got the call myself that year, and suddenly there was a peace within me. My future was planned, and I knew, for the first time, who I was supposed to be.

During my senior year, I was given a student teaching assignment—in my own junior high school. Memories of the Cougar Club party, cheerleading tryout rejections, and desegregation flooded my mind. But I was eager to begin and even more excited when I learned who my supervising teacher would be—Betty Whitfield, one of the best teachers in the school. Also, she had been in my mother's Sunday School class; I had known her nearly my entire life.

Mrs. Whitfield had the classroom management piece down to a science, of course, so I walked into an ideal situation. Even when she left the room and the students were alone with me, they behaved like angels. After all, they knew that Mrs. Whitfield was still in the building! I taught ninth graders *Romeo and Juliet* while we practiced our "Shakespeare's Word of the Day." I knew then that I had chosen a wonderful profession—not only was it easy, but I was able to talk about authors and books all day (and I could coach cheerleaders, too). Teaching was perfect for me.

Coming Down to Earth

Well, at least *student teaching* was perfect. It was so perfect, in fact, that I graduated from college with a false sense of confidence. I remember the bold way I walked into a school district's central office that June and asked to speak to a personnel director. The receptionist told me, "Fill out this application and mail it back." I took it, walked across the parking lot to my car, and stopped dead in my tracks.

"No!" I shouted to no one in particular. "I'm not leaving without a job!" I marched back into the building to the same receptionist and asked her to give me a list of the names of the high school principals. She smirked and announced that I wouldn't be able to reach any of them—they were all in a meeting room right behind me. I thanked her, turned and walked to the door leading to that room, and waited. After an hour, the door opened, and I jumped in front of the first person I saw.

"I want a job!" I declared to an alarmed principal and everyone else within earshot. In August, he was my boss.

It turned out that getting a job was the easy part. It wasn't long before my newly acquired self-assurance was waning, and I wondered what had possessed me to go back into that building that day. I remember meeting my colleagues for the first time. I scanned over a crowd of them as we boarded a school bus to attend a districtwide convocation, and wondered if I had anything in common with these veteran educators. As luck would have it, the first available seat on the bus was with another English teacher. As I sat down to introduce myself, the teacher looked at me and in a deep, resonant voice asked, "For whom does your husband work?" I must have sat there for a full minute with my mouth agape. I had only recently gotten rid of the "ain'ts" and double negatives that were commonplace in my neighborhood conversations. Immediately I felt out of place and certainly not worthy to teach a class that would require such formality with language.

And once we returned to the school, I couldn't believe that it took me five teacher workdays to get something as simple as the bulletin board displays ready for the first day of school. In those days there were no prefabricated borders or letters made for teachers, so I sat there, by myself, for five long days and cut letters. I had decided to divide one board into two sections: one section would say "Literature"; the other would say "Grammar." The problem was that one section said "Literature" and one read "Grammer." Some teacher I had never seen before walked by my door on that last workday and said, "You spelled that wrong" and continued down the hallway. I was devastated! I was a high school English teacher who had misspelled a word! Please understand: if there's one thing I can do, it's spell. My relationship with math ended somewhere around tenth-grade algebra and the time I scored a three on a test. But spelling has always been a strength. Perhaps I was weary from all that cutting, but that mistake seemed like an omen. I wondered if I would ever make it as a teacher.

A Rude Awakening

Once the students arrived, I realized I really wasn't prepared to teach. When I was calling the roll the first day, a senior stood up, arms outstretched, and looked around at his classmates: "Obviously, she doesn't know who I am."

> *"I don't care who you are," I asserted, trying to be in charge. "Sit down!" Things went rapidly downhill from there.*

"I don't care who you are," I asserted, trying to be in charge. "Sit down!" Things went rapidly downhill from there.

Drug deals were consummated in my classroom right under my nose, and I didn't even realize it. Once I saw large sums of money being passed back and forth, and when I asked about it, the students said, "Oh, we're taking up for a field trip." Later, I was called to the principal's office and told that those students had been suspended for selling drugs at school.

"Didn't you notice anything?" he asked.

"No," I answered, my head hanging down. "They were just taking up field trip money."

"Why would students be collecting money instead of a teacher?" was the next question, and of course I didn't have an answer.

There were other surprises. That year was the first time I had ever been sworn at and the first time I became aware that some students choose not to complete work, choose to fail. I was horrified.

And though I tried to motivate them to be successful, I found that my students fell into one of two categories: those who were argumentative and confrontational and those who wanted to be "friends" with the new, young teacher. I remember being challenged on virtually every assignment I gave: "That's too hard" or "This is too easy; we did it last year." Meanwhile, I was continually invited to high school parties and even the prom. No matter how important the job was to me, I was not taken seriously.

And to be honest, I'm sure I didn't have the demeanor of a teacher who wanted to be taken seriously. I certainly felt out of place as a twenty-two-year-old in the teacher's lounge. It seemed that many of my colleagues were my mother's age, and their main topics of conversation centered around recipes and Tupperware parties. At the same time, I would overhear my seniors talk about *real* parties, and here I was fresh out of college. It's not difficult to understand why I struggled to have the presence of an instructional leader. I sure didn't feel like one.

Instructionally, I was a mess. The lessons I had used as a junior high student teacher were not appropriate for high school English. There were no mentors for new teachers back then, so I walked a few steps down to a colleague's room to ask for help. "I don't know what to teach," I confessed. She handed me a textbook, pointed to a few pages, and closed her door.

One day I sat on my desk as I read aloud to the class. Another teacher walked by my door, stuck her head in, and said, "You'll learn not to do that" and walked away in a huff. Do what? I thought. Read? That was the only piece of advice I got from a fellow teacher that year.

When I look back at those instructional practices now, I shudder with regret. There were daily worksheets, skill-and-drill grammar exercises, and reading assignments that had little or no connection to my students. I had two classes of students who had been identified as gifted, and I remember looking over their research papers and having no clue as to how to grade them for content. They were too difficult for me to read! One student wrote about nuclear physics; all I could do was look for punctuation errors. On many occasions I felt that I should be teaching my students *more,* but I didn't know where to begin.

Still, I put a great deal of time into my job. I taught five different levels of English and one drama class. I was the cheerleading coach, the Pep Club sponsor, and the Drama Club coach. I directed the spring talent show and assisted with the spring musical. Most days I arrived at 7:30 and left late at night after practices and ball games. When that school year ended, in June 1980, I was exhausted.

My yearbook picture as cheerleading coach in 1979—my first year teaching.

Soon after, I received a letter saying enrollment was down at my school, and because I was the last person hired, I would be moved to a school across town for the next year. The thought of another first year in a new school with all new faculty, administration, and students was too much to bear.

I resigned.

I wouldn't enter a classroom again for seven years. During those years I moved to another town, worked at a dance studio (continuing my cheerleader dream), had children, suffered the end of a marriage, and often wondered about the career that I had given up.

But I had learned a lesson years before, on that night I was cut from cheerleading. You work hard, do the best you can, and, when you get knocked down, you pick yourself up, dust yourself off, and start over.

And that's what I did.

The Class I Lost

In fall 1987, I became a single parent who needed a job with benefits. I called the school system's central office and signed up to become a substitute teacher. All substitutes were required to attend a three-day training that offered classroom management hints and lesson plans. I was amazed at how the memories of my teaching days came flooding back during the workshop, and that I was so eager to begin.

I was called almost immediately to substitute in a seventh-grade classroom. I entered the building that morning excited to be back in a school. Something about it felt so comfortable, so "me." I read over the teacher's lesson plan for the day and was surprised to see that I was to take the class outside to the playground once they completed their worksheets. I was even more surprised to see the first class finish the work in five minutes. I said, "Your teacher says that when you're finished you can . . ."

My voice trailed off because the students were leaving the room. I quickly gathered the keys to the classroom and headed out to follow the class. I stepped into the hallway and looked left and right. They were gone. I thought they must have known the routine and headed for the playground, so I headed there too.

There was not a student to be seen.

I went back into the building and started looking around. I checked the bathrooms, the cafeteria, under the stairwells. No students. The problem was that I was looking for people I didn't know, complete strangers I had seen for a total of five minutes. I didn't know what they were wearing or who they were. And I had lost them.

I'll never forget walking into the school office that morning to tell the principal that I had lost my class.

I'll never forget walking into the school office that morning to tell the principal that I had lost my class. I think he was amused, though concerned, and before we could decide what to do, the bell for the next period rang. We looked at each other knowingly: the students would now be heading to their second-period class, to a real teacher who knew their names. I returned to the classroom and changed the lesson plans. There would be no playground time for the remainder of that day, and I had to be creative to contain a simmering pot of teenagers who finished their worksheets in five minutes. So we had some dancing, some singing, and some joke telling to fill the class time. Initially the students were reluctant; they weren't too sure about the singing substitute. But soon they responded to my teaching style, and I felt that maybe my teaching instincts were working. I knew then that I wanted to have a class of my own again—at least that way I would know the students' names.

The Class I Couldn't Teach

In February 1988, I returned to teaching. There was an opening in an eighth-grade language arts class, and I thought, *Junior high can't be so tough.* I had taught high school, after all. No one had warned me about the hazards of starting a teaching job in the middle of the year, though. The students were the first to tell me that they had run off three teachers already—and that they had terrorized substitutes for a month (visions of lost students danced in my head).

I had never seen behavior problems like these before. These students did not sit down! They walked around the classroom constantly, looking out the window, punching each other, and totally disregarding me. It was as if I weren't even there. They had me so rattled I mispronounced words—and they laughed at me.

My return to teaching probably looked like those fictional classrooms we sometimes see on television shows and movies—disruptive students walking around the room ignoring the teacher, wads of paper being used as projectiles, and students yelling out the windows to passersby. I was horrified to find myself a player in the real-life version of this scenario.

I immediately did the same thing I had done as a first-year teacher. I asked for help. I sat down in my principal's office and

31

asked him why he had failed to mention that I would be teaching the spawn of Satan for four months. He smiled a great big smile and told me that because I was young (he also said "pretty," but I think he was just buttering me up so he wouldn't lose his fourth teacher to the spawn), I would have to try harder to gain respect. He also told me that he knew exactly what would help me—a class observation. This was news to me. As a first-year teacher, no adult had ever entered my classroom. But at this school, the administrator would come in, watch me teach, take a few notes, and fix everything! I wasn't sure I believed in that system, but I knew one thing for sure: as long as an administrator was in the room, that would be a period of time when I wouldn't be alone with those kids.

I still have that first evaluation:

Instructional Presentation—At Standard

    Adapts work to student needs. Needs to closely follow

        six-step lesson plan. (I had neither seen nor heard of a six-

        step lesson plan.)

Management of Instructional Time—Below Standard

    Needs to maintain high time on task (I didn't know what "on

        task" meant. I just wanted them to spend "high time" in

        their seats.)

Instructional Feedback—At Standard

    Good feedback given on in-class work. (They did work that

        day?)

Management of Student Behavior—Below Standard

    Needs to consistently enforce established rules within class.

        (Ya think?!)

Interacting Within the Educational Environment—Above Standard

    Wants the best for all students. (Yes, I did.)

In my defense, I had been out of teaching for seven years, and I was unaware of the standards for these evaluations. But looking back on that year, I'm not surprised that my observation reflected so poorly on me as a teacher. I remember going to the office to ask how many sick days I had been given for the remainder of the year. I took that number and divided it by the weeks I had left. I wanted to figure out a way that I could take one sick day every week so I would have to face those classes only four days at a time.

That year was one of the most stressful teaching years I ever endured. However, it was the last year I was ever given a "Below Standard" on an evaluation. Years later, after we were reunited, I asked Mrs. Warnecke how she had been such a good beginning teacher. "I thought I wasn't," she replied. "I really didn't think I knew what I was doing that year. I had taught high school social studies my first year, and once I became a first-grade teacher, they expected me to teach everything—art, music, reading. I felt very lost and unprepared."

Years later, after we were reunited, I asked Mrs. Warnecke how she had been such a good teacher. "I thought I wasn't," she replied. "I really didn't think I knew what I was doing that year."

Lost describes exactly where I was that year. I knew that I had to find myself as a teacher, however difficult it might be. And even after such a rough beginning, I was still determined to do it, and I started the very next year.

✿ "May each of us think of the other . . ."
—B. WARNECKE, JUNE 1967

THREE

Finding the Connections

I have a mantra. Actually, I have several, but one thing I tell new teachers over and over is this: *if you make them the enemy, you will lose.* I thought of some kids as the enemy during my first two years, and I lost. I lost respect from my colleagues, I lost sleep, I lost confidence in myself as a teacher. I just plain lost.

When that student mouthed off on my first day of teaching, bringing his classmates along for the ride, my response immediately fostered a "me vs. them" mentality in my class. I struggled that entire year to overcome it. In my second year of teaching, I wasn't much better. The student who laughed at me when I stumbled over the words "past participle" and yelled out, "Say it right!" joined the minions of hell in my mind that very moment, and stayed there.

In my third year of teaching, something gradually started to happen. What was at first a tiny flicker of realization grew larger and larger, somewhat like the Grinch's heart. I began to understand that my students brought their own self-esteem issues to school and often acted out in an effort to get attention, *any* kind of attention, even if it was negative. I discovered that relating to those students, maybe seeing a bit of myself in them, was a way to make my classroom less of a battlefield. The feeling became more "we're in this together" than me against them. Even more important, it was during this year that I realized it was OK for me to actually *care* about my students.

Starting Over

I waited eagerly for the first day of school that year. I would be teaching an elective drama and dance class, and I was so excited that I wasn't even disappointed that my classroom was a dilapidated trailer beside the faculty parking lot. I knew that this time I would have my own classes from the first day of school, and that this surely would make a difference. No more substitute teachers there before me, just me with my first-day-of-school expectations all ready to be delivered. As the first-period bell was about to ring, I walked up the steps of that rickety trailer. The railing on the porch was hanging by one rusty nail, and I was trying to reconnect it when I saw my first students approaching. Two girls were running toward me, arguing loudly with each other. Finally, they stopped in front of the trailer, and one of them announced, "Miss Lady, LaShawn just called me a VIRGIN!"

Startled, I opened my mouth to say something about sticks and stones, but instead I mumbled, "You're in the eighth grade. What's wrong with being called a virgin?"

She looked at me as if she couldn't believe what I had just said. "Because it AIN'T TRUE!!!" she yelled and then ran toward the parking lot. I sent the other girl, who had the goofiest grin I've ever seen, to bring Miss "I'm Not a Virgin" back. When they returned, I counseled LaShawn about name-calling. The entire time I was talking to her, she kept grinning at me. Sometimes the grin turned into full-fledged laughter, and soon I was having a hard time keeping a straight face myself.

That turned out to be pretty much par for the course. LaShawn *bounced* into the trailer every day—I never saw her walk. She'd jump the three trailer steps, bounce into the room, and say the same thing, day after day: "Can I go to the store?"—referring to the convenience store across the street. And every day I would tell her that *of course* she couldn't leave campus to walk across the street. Then LaShawn would take two marching steps and plant her feet shoulder-width apart in two loud stomps. As soon as the trailer stopped rattling, she would raise her arm straight up in the air, Statue of Liberty style, and then announce, "Er-y day, er-y day, I ask you if I, LaShawn Williamson, can go to the store, and er-y day, you say 'No!' " Then she would sit down and look straight ahead, a determined pout on her face. I always stifled my laughter and tried to remain professional, but with difficulty. Eventually, I would be able to say, "OK, LaShawn, let's get to work."

Gradually it became clear to me that I loved that child. From the minute LaShawn bounced into that trailer until class was over and she bounced out, I knew that it could actually be fun to teach. And that affection started spilling over to other students in that class, who laughed at LaShawn's routine just as I did, and into my other classes. We would work some, laugh some, and work some more. I even began to feel comfortable touching the students; a light pat on the shoulder was a gesture I had never attempted as a beginning teacher. Soon my classes felt more like a family, and I looked forward to seeing them every day.

The same year LaShawn was delivering her daily speech in my trailer, I taught Wendy, a frail girl with translucently pale skin. In November she told me she was pregnant. I couldn't believe that it was possible, that I would be teaching someone who was going to have a baby. My own children weren't much older than babies themselves. But after the winter break it was obvious that she was indeed pregnant, and as time went on, she couldn't fit comfortably at her desk. I bought a beanbag chair for her, and it wasn't long before I had to help her get out of it at the end of class.

Some days I let her stay a little after the bell so we could talk. I listened to her tell me how important the baby was to her, how much she loved the father, and how they were going to have a life together. Later I held a sobbing eighth grader after the baby came early and didn't make it. Not long after, the father left her, too. She told me that she wouldn't even come to school if it weren't for my class. That was the only place she felt that she could be herself and not be judged. I knew then that I was teaching so much more than dance and drama.

I began to understand that accepting all my students, regardless of the misfortunes they dealt with on a daily basis, would be the key to being able to teach them effectively.

As time went on, little by little I recognized the importance of establishing and nurturing relationships with the students in my classroom. I was particularly drawn to adolescents who struggled with their self-confidence, for reasons that are clear to me now, but weren't at the time. I don't know why I wasn't able to pull from my memories of first grade—and Mrs. Warnecke's unconditional acceptance of me—earlier in my career, but I did begin to understand that accepting *all* my students, regardless of the misfortunes they dealt with on a daily basis, would be the key to being able to teach them effectively. And as my relationships with my students developed, I knew that I was not only teaching but also learning.

Take the case of Curtis, for example. He was a big guy, a football player, who always had a polite smile when he entered my first-period classroom. One day, though, he came in spouting negative comments at everyone around him—including me. Understanding that this was totally out of character for Curtis, I talked to him and decided against sending him to the office. But he was also rude to his next-period teacher, and then I had another run-in with him in the cafeteria, over something as insignificant as his place in the lunch line. Finally, I told him that I was going to have to write a discipline referral on him, and that he could just go ahead to the office.

"You don't even care that my daddy died last night!" Curtis yelled. I was stunned. My first thought was to wonder why he was even at school, but next I knew that I had learned a valuable lesson. As a teacher, I have to be aware of the many variables that influence student behavior. I certainly thought that I was sensitive enough to recognize a problem, but that day with Curtis reminded me that Mrs. Warnecke had treated each student with a sensitivity that I was still trying to develop as a teacher.

This brings me to Kenton.

Orange People Pictures

Kenton was in my homeroom and first-period class one year when I was teaching seventh-grade language arts; I had the pleasure of starting my day with him every day. I have always been close to students in my homeroom because we spend so much time together. On picture day, I take my homeroom to the auditorium and encourage them to smile; on testing days, I bring biscuits for a classroom breakfast and throw "smarty vibes" at them by wiggling my fingers as though I'm casting a "spell" of correct answers. They're my report card distribution kids and my cumulative folder kids. It's common to become attached to those students. Kenton, however, didn't let anyone get close to him. First of all, he came into the school angry almost every day. He would come through the door yelling about his bus driver.

"Mrs. Rigsbee! I got kicked off the bus again," he would declare to the world. Of course I would immediately ask what had happened this time.

"He lied on me again!" Kenton would then grab a desk, push it, and watch it skate across the floor with a grinding screech. Here's the thing about middle schools: they're full of liars. And evidently they're also filled with thieves. Kenton never had a pencil. Not one day. So every day he would ask me for a pencil.

"Kenton," I would implore. "Where is the pencil I gave you yesterday?"

"Somebody stole it."

"Where was it?" (For some reason, I felt compelled to continue to interrupt instruction for this conversation.)

"In my locker."

"Didn't you have a lock on your locker?" (Why must I continue to distract the other twenty-nine students from working?)

"Yeah," he would continue, unconcerned. "Somebody knows my combination."

OK, I'll bite. "Did you give someone your combination?"

"No. They peeped over my shoulder while I was opening my locker."

Kenton and I would have similar conversations every day, and one day I had seriously had enough. He started the day angry at his bus driver as usual. He got my entire homeroom agitated and then settled himself and asked for a pencil. I said, "Kenton, I don't have a pencil. And you know what? There are no more pencils in the office. In fact, there are no pencils left in the United States of America, and there are NO MORE TREES!"

Unmoved, he just reached over to my supply table and picked up an orange marker. I thought *OK, fine. I don't care. As long as he does his work, it can be done in marker.* So I continued to teach, and periodically I would notice Kenton writing. I didn't look closely at his paper at first. But I could have: from the first day of school, Kenton's assigned seat was in the "smackin' row."

(Obviously, I don't smack my students. But at the time I affectionately called the row of desks that runs along the front of the room the "smackin' row" because I told students that those are the desks I can reach from the front. I would say, "You'd better do your work because you're in the smackin' row, and I can reach you from here." In contrast, the seats in the back of the room are in the "Go Go Gadget arm row," a reference to the cartoon character Inspector Gadget who has bionic limbs and can stretch his arms to great distances. The smackin' row was both a joke and a term of endearment for those kids strategically selected to sit in front. Lately I have become more sensitive; the first row is now the "laying on of the hands row." But when I had Kenton, I was still "smackin'.")

Eventually I walked over, while continuing my lesson, to get a look at his orange marker work. When I saw his paper, my heart sank. Kenton was not doing the work. He was drawing orange stick people.

I don't think I can adequately express the feeling that came over me at this time. All I know is that it started at my toes and worked its way up. By the time it got to my mouth, I was leaning over the smackin' seat and growling, loudly, "KENTON!" He didn't raise his head but merely shifted his eyes to look up at me.

At that point, I had a decision to make. I stood hovering over him and thought about all of the things I could say. I could have broken his spirit. I could have gone into a diatribe about how he always came to class angry and never had a pencil and never did any work. But somehow, in that moment, I saw little first-grade Cindy, and it was as if a voice spoke in my ears, asking *What would Mrs. Warnecke do?*

And suddenly I knew what I had to do. I took a deep breath and spoke: "Kenton, [breathe] those are the most beautiful orange stick people I've ever seen." The class let out a collective sigh of relief. Kenton smiled up at me, and at that very minute, things changed. I received what became known as Orange People Pictures for the rest of the year. Kenton started to do his work—with the orange marker—and every day I would accept it, praise him, and grade the paper along with everyone else's. Nearing the end of the year, Kenton's work, all in the form of Orange People Pictures, decorated every wall of my room.

After a final field trip that year, we stopped at a local mall so that the students could eat lunch at the food court. Kenton was in my group, and some of us walked around the mall while waiting for the others to finish eating. I was the first in the group to approach an art display in the center court of the mall, and after closer inspection, I realized that it was a school district art display—each art teacher from every school in our district had submitted student work. I couldn't believe my eyes when I saw an eighteen-by-twenty-four-inch Orange People Picture!

I couldn't speak. My chin trembled. "Kenton," I mumbled. "Kenton. There's your picture."

"Yeah," he replied. "The art teacher likes 'em, too."

I thought back to the day when I made that all-important decision to give Kenton unconditional acceptance through a compliment on his artwork—the same treatment I had received as a first-grade poet so many years before. And I thought about how one comment changed him from an angry seventh grader into a hard worker who wanted to please the teacher. Clearly, it had been the right decision.

Mrs. Venit and Mrs. Helfand

Mrs. Venit and Mrs. Helfand, I will never forget the impression you had upon me in the art classes I had with you. Both of you lit the fire in me to make my mark as an artist and ultimately as an art teacher. As a young boy I was impressed by your skills in drawing. I therefore aspired to be able to draw like you. Seeing that I had an early interest in drawing, one of you gave me a book filled with pen-and-ink illustrations of dinosaurs (I am sorry to say I don't remember which of you this was—maybe you do?). I happily drew every dinosaur in that book.

The years were 1966–67; in those days junior high school included seventh and eighth grades, and I believe I had each of you that same school year. What you two ladies did was amazing to me. Mrs. Venit, you had the ability to write your name simultaneously with each hand—right hand writing in the normal direction—left to right—and the left hand writing right to left. To this day I have never figured out how you did that.

Mrs. Helfand, you taught me how to draw the human figure by breaking down each part of the body into basic geometrical parts just like the mannequins art students use as teaching aides and props. You then had our art class's best drawers execute a mural that graced the hallways in the lobby where our trophy cases were located. My part was a drawing/painting of a basketball game scene—can you remember that?

Those two experiences have stayed with me to this very day, and I thank you both, Mrs. Helfand and Mrs. Venit, two unforgettable art teachers I had at Van Wyck Junior High School 217 in Queens, New York City, New York (Class of 1967). Thanks for those positive and lifelong learning experiences.

—Edney L. Freeman, comprehensive academics 9–12, Charlotte Amalie High School, St. Thomas, Virgin Islands, 2009 U.S. Virgin Islands Teacher of the Year

A New Understanding

So, beginning with my third year of teaching and onward through my career, I saw the importance of developing relationships with my students. But it would take a few years before I would fully understand the effect of those relationships on my students. Somewhere around my fifth year of teaching, the letters started coming. They trickled in slowly at first, but steadily; year after year, they came.

Because of a city-county school merger, I was teaching in a different school when I looked up one day to see Keshia, a student I had taught years before, standing in my classroom staring at me. I had worked hard to establish a relationship with the child, who had some issues with authority figures, even after she confronted me in the girls' bathroom one day and called me a "Miss America Bitch." I didn't know what she meant by the "Miss America" part; I certainly understood the rest. But on this day, she'd come in to tell me that her high school teacher had given her class an assignment to write a letter to a teacher who had "made a difference." Reading her letter, I was astonished. Until that point, I hadn't known that my former students even remembered me.

Keshia had written three pages, in a beautiful cursive hand.

> You taught me to use my mind instead of my fists. You guided me through the hard paths of school and of life. If I ever had a student like me, I don't think I would take the time that you took with me. . . . I am sorry for all of the pain I put you through. But people no longer look at me and frown. In fact, sometimes they smile. I owe most of that to you. I'll never forget all you've done for me.

I still remember vividly where I was standing in my classroom, mouth agape, when I read those words.

Two days later a letter came from another student in that same high school classroom: "My teacher told us to write to the teacher who had influenced us the most, and I immediately thought of you. . . . You cared about people and respected their feelings."

Finally, it seemed, I was starting to understand what I was supposed to be doing as a teacher. The evidence that I was making connections that persisted years later was incredible validation. I "cared about people" just as Mrs. Warnecke had cared about me, and they knew it.

Finally, it seemed, I was starting to understand what I was supposed to be doing as a teacher.

Sometimes, though, building those relationships took extra work. One year I had a seventh-grade language arts class that was very difficult to get focused on instruction. It was a small class, fourteen very lively boys and one girl, Tenisha. Tenisha tried to hold her own in that classroom, but despite her feistiness, those boys let her know who was boss. Demario and Imhotep were artists and sat at their desks sketching continuously. They were good at it, too. Cerrone had a little song that he sang over and over. It went like this: "Do do dodo dodo . . ." Whenever there was a silent moment—for example, if I tried to take a breath while teaching—Cerrone would sing out, "Do do dodo dodo!" Jonathan, the biggest seventh grader I ever taught, was a football player the team referred to as Earthquake. He was extremely shy and very quiet, and the other guys liked to bounce off of him—literally. They would throw their bodies against his and bounce off! It was the highlight of the class period as they entered class and as they left— bouncing off the Earthquake.

So it wasn't surprising that I had a hard time keeping this very active class in line to walk to the lunchroom. We had to walk outside the school building to get to the cafeteria door, and all the way these boys would run, jump, kick, tumble, and play while Tenisha and I followed along. It was not uncommon for Cerrone to smack Imhotep and then take off running with the other boys in chase. But one day I had an idea. I asked the principal if I could develop an incentive program for this class, and she agreed. If the students brought materials to class, completed all their work, and walked nicely to and from the cafeteria on Monday through

Thursday, on Fridays I would take them to the food court at the mall for lunch.

I came up with an intricate classroom behavior chart, and although it was hard work documenting every child's behavior every day, it worked! There was a turnaround in behavior, and student achievement soared. Those kids loved going to the mall on Fridays— maybe even as much as I did! I would drive them over in the school's activity van, and we'd be back at the end of the lunch period.

Because this class was my "lunch bunch," we became very close. Soon we were taking weekend trips to movies and ball games, too. Once again I recognized the difference those all-important relationships make. I loved those kids, and, just as important, I loved teaching because my classroom was no longer a battlefield.

A Surprise Announcement

That same year, my seventh year of teaching, was a monumental one for me for many reasons. In addition to my successful, albeit unorthodox, incentive program, to my surprise I was voted the Teacher of the Year for my school.

As soon as I heard the news, I walked to my colleague's classroom to make sure I wasn't imagining that I had heard my name on the afternoon announcements. She laughed and told me that she herself had nominated me because of my relationships with the kids and because I worked so hard. I was honored, of course, and excited that the faculty of my school had recognized that I was giving so much of myself to my job and my kids, but I was a little nervous when I found out what was to come. The honor came with a classroom visit from the school district's Teacher of the Year selection committee. They would not only observe my teaching but also stay in my school the entire day, talking to staff members and students about me and my teaching.

When I shared that information with my colleagues, they all had the same comment: "They're going to see your fourth-period class!" Teachers offered to take a few of the lunch bunch for the period, but I wanted the experience to be genuine. I told them I'd keep everyone, and we would go on as if it were a regular school day.

My fourth-period class was the most upset of all. "But we can't behave!" they cried.

"We can't even be quiet," Cerrone said, and added, "Do do dodo dodo."

I told them we would be fine, and turned around to the board to write. But something was wrong—the class was totally silent. There was no talking, there were no pencils scraping across paper to make a masterpiece, there was no singing. I was scared to turn around.

Slowly, I turned and looked. And then my eyes welled up with tears. All of my students had taped their mouths shut. (Later, I learned that Cerrone had grabbed the masking tape off my desk and the class had passed it around.) I asked them to take off the tape. Only Cerrone did.

"We're practicing trying to keep quiet, Mrs. Rigsbee. We can do this when the judges are in the room, too!"

"Now, Cerrone, what do you think the judges will think if they come in here and my whole class is taped up?"

Cerrone sang his little song again.

I was not nervous on the day the judges came. I had been nervous before, especially during the interviews, but now they were here in *my* classroom with *my* children. I just wanted them to see how I had worked to teach those fifteen children to be better readers. I had taught them strategies to help them interact with text and raise their level of comprehension. And I had done it with the help of my most important teaching tool—relationships.

I had taught them strategies to help them interact with text and raise their level of comprehension. And I had done it with the help of my most important teaching tool—relationships.

As I planned my lesson for the special day, I laminated several pictures from a magazine. On the day the visitors sat in my classroom, I asked my students to look at the pictures and then brainstorm ideas for a description paper. One by one, I held the pictures up and asked the students to describe them.

When it was Jonathan's turn, I displayed a picture of a festive multicolored hot air balloon, though I immediately wished I had chosen a better selection for him—maybe a sports picture, something more masculine; I didn't want to make him uncomfortable. But the picture was already up there for the class, and the committee, to see, so I moved on.

"Jonathan, how would you describe this?" I asked.

Jonathan struggled, cleared his throat, coughed, and looked at his feet. We all waited. The class looked at Jonathan, then the judges, then at me . . . as if to say, "Answer. Answer anything!"

Slowly, Jonathan, the Earthquake, looked up at me and said, in a barely audible voice, "It's, uh, it's . . . a pear-shaped rainbow."

The room fell silent. Tenisha gasped. The other boys whispered under their breaths, "Yes! Yes!" I had tears in my eyes when I said, "Jonathan, that's a beautiful description."

I will never forget that moment. I will always remember the bunch of rowdy boys who taped their mouths for me and the big, quiet boy who came up with one of the best metaphors I've ever heard.

Later, when I told my class that I had been named the District Teacher of the Year, over the cheers and the shouts, I heard a voice singing, "Do do dodo dodo," a tune that rings in my memory to this day.

My "lunch bunch" class with me at a college football game. Cerrone's in the middle, probably singing his song.

Getting to Know You

Since the year I taught my lunch bunch class, I've made a commitment to really get to know my students. Every school year I begin with the same assignment: "In your journal, write an entry that begins 'The worst thing that ever happened to me was . . .'" This one assignment tells me more about my students than almost anything else we do all year. One year I had an entire class who wrote entries that sounded like, "The worst thing that ever happened to me was when I saw my brother get shot." I knew early that that year was going to be a difficult one. I had to work hard to establish trust; my students were angry and full of despair, and there were days when I wondered if I was even making a difference.

The next year I had an entirely different group of students. The journal entries that year sounded like this: "The worst thing that ever happened to me is when my mom took my television out of my room." Believe it or not, those kids were just as difficult to reach. Most of them didn't feel the need to be close to the teacher; they were fulfilled at home and found school to be merely a place to hang out with their friends. Eventually, I was able to reach both groups, though, using some of the same strategies: humor, a little bit of insanity, and a dusting of "magic."

"All kinds of things may be the special key that unlocks the door. There is no way of knowing which one it will be, but like a janitor with a huge key ring, you just keeping trying until one fits."

—B. WARNECKE, JANUARY 1, 2009

FOUR

Exploring the Magic

As the years go by, I continue to find more and more evidence of how vital good student-teacher relationships are to students' success in school. At the same time, though, I've found that that connection by itself is not enough. Yes, Mrs. Warnecke had cared for her students, but I had many caring teachers during my school years. Another question I started to consider in my third year of teaching was, what was the difference between those teachers' classes and Mrs. Warnecke's?

Teaching can be a claustrophobic proposition, regardless of whether it's happening in a trailer, a state-of-the-art classroom, or a below-ground improvisation like my first-grade room. Here we teachers are, grown adults, but still governed by bells that tell us when to arrive, when we can leave, and when we can attend to personal needs. (I sometimes refer to my colleagues and myself as "Pavlov's Teachers" because we respond so well to bells.) The broken-down trailer I taught in during my third year was particularly claustrophobic. It was no more than twelve feet wide by about twenty feet long. Its entire length was lined with windows—in various states of functionality—which gave a view of the parking lot, the railroad tracks on the far side, and beyond that the roofs of the little town where I was teaching. I would stand in the room, look at the bell tower of the town hall in the distance, and think, *The world is out there, and I'm in here.*

One day, standing gazing out in my usual reverie, I started to think about how my students must feel. Middle and high school students have six or seven classes a day where they sit in uncomfortable desks for hours at a time. Even though many teachers work hard to engage their classes, it has to be difficult for the kids to be there. If it's hard for adults, who've had so much practice at it, it must be that much harder for young people.

Yet, thinking back on my school days and to the windowless basement where I attended first grade, I remembered it as a *magical* place—much more than four walls, rickety desks, and a blackboard. There must be, I thought, some way to recreate that feeling. And so I began that year to test some ideas for making the classroom a place where kids would want to be—a room like Mrs. Warnecke's.

Later on, after I left the language arts classroom and became a reading resource teacher, the issue of environment became even more critical to me. I realized that if I wanted students to be successful in my class, they needed to come there willingly. After all, I would be pulling them from other classes; they might be missing basketball or band or art—something they loved. Further, the stigma of a remedial reading class is always a concern. So over time I've come up with ways to make my classroom a special place, and I guess they work: my principal, Jason Johnson, said to me once, "I've never seen so many students beg to go to a reading class."

I thought, *I'm trying to make it magical in here . . .*

Here's what I've learned in twenty years about making the classroom a place kids want to be.

Breaking Down the Walls

To alleviate claustrophobia, I try as often as possible to get the students out of the classroom. Teachers know that learning is about discovery, and there's more to discover outside a school building than in it. Students have given me beautifully written descriptions of spider webs, flowers, blades of grass, clouds—it would be difficult to find that creativity inside four walls. Last year, for example, after we took a walk on a trail in the woods behind our school, my student Savannah wrote in her journal, "The skinny twig hung off the branch as if it were asleep." I didn't see Savannah's twig that day, but I can see it now.

Every year, I begin my writing instruction by taking my classes outside for an exercise in sensory writing. I tell my students that they are going to use all their senses except one—the sense of sight. I assign partners and loosely blindfold one student in each pair. The partners lead each other around the schoolyard as they listen to and feel everything around them. Once they are back in the classroom, they write reflections on their experiences, like this one of Brian's, a seventh grader:

> I was walking and trying to feel my way around the schoolyard. I felt the roughness of the bark on a tree, but I couldn't concentrate because I was nervous about falling or walking into the street. It made me appreciate the sense of sight even more than I already do, and it seems like concentrating on the way a piece of bark feels made me understand it in a different way.

I once taught at a school that sat beside an old cemetery. In the fall, I would take my classes out there to do gravestone rubbings so that the students could better determine what had long ago been carved into those weathered stones. Placing a piece of notebook paper against the gravestone, the students rubbed a pencil or crayon back and forth across the paper, and the names, dates, and other inscriptions magically appeared on the paper. My students were always thrilled and fascinated to see words on their papers that were illegible on the stone itself.

That cemetery had a long row of gravestones, seven in all, that appeared to be the graves of an entire family: parents and five of their children. We used these in a cross-curricular activity: after looking at the dates and doing the math to determine the children's ages when they died, my students would write beautiful stories about the family and how they lived in the seventeenth century.

I've always found getting the students out of the building to be a wonderful motivator, but it's certainly not an original idea. Pass by a school in the spring, and you'll see children all around, doing one activity or another in the sunshine. In my early years of teaching, I so wanted to be outside on the first warm day that I tried to be creative when thinking of activities that would match the learning goals for my class but could be done just as well out of the classroom.

Another way to escape the stuffiness of a classroom is to use the entire building whenever possible. My classes routinely do "reader's theatre" presentations in the auditorium—reading aloud the different characters' parts from a dramatic text—to an audience of one: me. The short walk from my classroom offers a change of scenery and loosens up the kids.

One year, after my class had turned in a particularly grueling research paper, I took them to the gym. There was only one rule. The entire class had to fit in the "jump ball" circle in the middle of the court. Once they got there, they could talk, scream, or dance, but they had to stay within the confines of the circle. The restriction ensured that the activity would be challenging, because the students were pressed against each other like a dozen clowns trying to cram into a Volkswagen. It was funny to see these middle school kids falling out of the circle but trying like crazy to stay in, and they loved it! The entire activity took only ten minutes, including traveling to and from the gym, but when we returned we were all more focused, having had the opportunity to "break down our walls" once again, while at the same time being a little silly.

Another twist on expanding the classroom is one I began while teaching summer school. Many times during my "summer career opportunities," I was teaching students who had displayed a strong work ethic throughout the year but still hadn't been able to pass their standardized tests. So, because it was summer and we had to be in a classroom, I told the students that we would be bringing our summer inside with us. On the classroom wall I wrote a poem (which was a little too reminiscent of my first-grade poetry):

> *All of our friends are out there*
> *in the world so wide.*
> *So since we want some summer, too,*
> *We'll just bring it all inside.*

Corny, I know. Still, around that poem on the wall we posted anything and everything "summer" that my students wanted to bring in. Some brought pictures of swimming pools and boats, some brought seashells, and others preferred to create their own artwork: drawings of flowers and summer scenes. At any time during my summer school classes, the students knew that they were allowed to go "get some summer" by taking a break in the back of the room. Even I got frustrated sometimes and headed back there myself. I would whine loudly, "I just want to be outside," and all the students would laugh at the crazy teacher who didn't want to spend her summer inside a classroom any more than her students did.

Walls with a Message

When I first started to reimagine what I wanted my classroom to be like, I made the most important and biggest test my own: Did I want to be there myself? If not, surely my students wouldn't. If I'm going to be in a classroom all day, I want it to be a pleasant place to be.

Fundamentals matter, of course. Twice I've painted my own classroom walls. (I even showed up once in the summer to paint the halls of the school!) But some teachers go to greater lengths. Beth, a sixth-grade science teacher in my school one year, painted a mural of tropical fish that covered one entire wall of her classroom. Her students were so excited when they first saw it at Open House; they felt like the luckiest sixth graders in the building to be in that room.

When I first started to reimagine what I wanted my classroom to be like, I made the most important and biggest test my own: Did I want to be there myself? If not, surely my students wouldn't. If I'm going to be in a classroom all day, I want it to be a pleasant place to be.

Some would probably argue that this type of physical labor is not in a teacher's job description. But I have to say that any amount of personal attention I can give to my classroom and building makes it more meaningful to me to be there every day. And because many of my students live in deplorable situations, I've always wanted to ensure that they have the best possible environment when they're at school.

Fresh paint is only the beginning. Prefabricated borders for bulletin boards and the other classroom decorations available from teacher supply stores are well and good, if on the pricey side (clearly, someone is making a great deal of money selling these things), but they probably aren't terribly meaningful to students.

I have always remembered fondly that the decorations in Mrs. Warnecke's room were made by her—few companies were selling classroom supplies in 1963. She taught us how to tell time on a handmade clock she had drawn with a human face and hands, the latter affixed with brad fasteners. But after my first-year bulletin board spelling error, it was about four years into teaching before I attempted anything more artistic than "Welcome Back to School." I used to joke that my Welcome Back message was still on the board in April!

I've relaxed a little since then. One type of decoration I often use is what I call "story starters." I cover an entire wall with pictures of some kind (it varies from year to year), and when students get stuck for writing ideas, they can look at the wall to get a jump start. For instance, every day when my students enter the room, I have them begin with a warm-up activity. To get them focused I provide a prompt—a question or quotation—and the students respond in their journals. If they draw a blank, the wall is there for inspiration.

The first year I did story starters, I decided to use several posters of cute little babies that I had gathered. There were babies sitting in unrolled toilet paper, babies with food all over their faces, babies snuggling up to puppies. But there was a problem with these pictures—all the babies were white. In the back of my mind, I knew this was a problem when I hung the posters, but Open House was approaching, and I didn't want bare walls when the parents came to visit. Then I forgot about it until sometime in October, when one of my students, Brandon, asked me, "Mrs. Rigsbee, why don't you have any black babies up there?"

I wanted to crawl under the floor. I'd been thinking that I had finally gotten this teaching thing together, but I'd blown it again. I hadn't meant to be insensitive to the majority of my students, of course; I just hadn't been able to find any posters of black babies or Hispanic babies or Asian babies. I told Brandon that, and that I would continue looking. And I did, but as I had figured, there were none to be found. So one day I went in and pulled all the posters down.

Then I explained the problem to the students and asked for their help. For weeks afterward, they brought me pictures of babies—themselves as babies; their brothers, cousins, nieces, and nephews as babies; their neighbors' babies. It was a babyfest! And they loved writing their baby stories whenever they chose the story starter wall.

One year, I wanted to have a board that highlighted student poetry. So I cut out letters that read "Dive into POETRY." Then I asked Charlie, the best artist in the class, "What would be a cool picture to go with this?" Charlie got right to work, and the next day he came in with the cutest frog, long legs outstretched, jumping off a diving board (nicely placed on a lily pad) into a pond. After stapling Charlie's picture to the board, I added student poetry all around as the water. That board was a turning point for me in my attempt to make a classroom for and about the students. From that point on, I stopped buying classroom decorations from stores. I now use student work and projects, and we make our own wall designs every year. And student artists get a venue for showcasing their creations.

For the last two years, I have taken a large piece of bulletin board paper, ripped from the roll so that the edges are jagged and rough, and written "Reading Strategies We Use" on it. (I'm not an artist, so this is my idea of abstract art.) Then the students choose their own pieces of paper, also abstractly ripped, and they write strategies on them. We place all these on the wall, like a huge collage, and I point to it all year when talking about what we do when we read. I've also seen the students look at it while they read—it's a reading guide and artwork, all in one. It's colorful and decorative (not to mention cheap), and you can't find it in a teacher store. And because it's unique to my classroom and my students, it feels like ours, and makes us feel at home at school.

Mrs. Vail

Though it was decades ago, if I close my eyes, I can still see my kindergarten teacher, Mrs. Vail. Her classroom was a big, bright frenzy of huge paint jugs, stacks of vivid paper, and cups of colorful crayons. Every day her lucky students were excited, inspired, and creating . . . truly learning with joy and love.

During one memorable Show and Tell, Camille stood before the other boys and girls and slowly opened her brown paper bag. We all gasped as she held up the butterfly wings she had worn as part of her costume in a dance recital. The paper wings were glittery and perfect. Mrs. Vail watched as all ten of the girls sitting on the floor turned green with envy. But she never mentioned those feelings. She walked across the room, swung open her cabinet, and quickly scooped up some supplies. Our teacher sat in front of us and began chatting all about dancing and growing up, while her scissors flashed this way and that through a stack of pink, purple, and aqua tissue paper. She unrolled sheets of crepe paper, snapping her stapler here and there. Smiling at us, she called our names so we could all be fitted with a beautiful pair of butterfly wings. Mrs. Vail walked us out to the green hills in back of school so we could run about and flutter our wings behind us.

Two things I remember about that day: school is a place where beautiful and magical things are created, and teachers have superhuman abilities in their hands and hearts.

—Jeanne Muzi, first-grade teacher, Benjamin Franklin Elementary School, Lawrenceville, New Jersey, 2009 New Jersey Teacher of the Year

Creating Adventure

There has been some discussion about whether an overly decorated room might be distracting to students who have Attention Deficit Hyperactivity Disorder (ADHD). As a parent of a child diagnosed with ADHD and a teacher of many students diagnosed with the disorder, I am familiar with this notion, but not once in my career have I had to redirect a student from staring at a wall. What I have seen, instead, are students who say, "This room is cool! I wish my class was in here!"

In an elementary school classroom I visited once, the teacher had fashioned, out of bulletin board paper, a three-dimensional "cave" that surrounded her classroom door. To get into the room, everyone, adults included, had to get on their knees and climb through the cave door. Inside the room were computers placed in tents and animals in terrariums and cages. I asked a student how he liked the class. He replied, "It's not a class. It's an adventure." I knew at that moment that I wanted my classroom to be an adventure, too.

So a few years ago, when I was setting up my reading classroom, that's the feeling I was going for. I started by choosing a theme. I decided that because reading "takes you places," I would use the Dr. Seuss book *Oh, the Places You'll Go!* as the motif. I bought colorful, spongy letters about four inches high that spelled out "OH, THE PLACES WE'LL GO" and hung them across the back wall of my room. Then I placed colorful ABC-patterned cloth over my tables—I just walked into a fabric store, and there it was, a beautiful corduroy fabric that matched the primary colors of the letters.

Next, I went on eBay and purchased a red tent and set it up in the room. Elsewhere in the room I set up a cozy area with a chair, shelves, a reading light, and a rug. A beach chair, towel, and sand bucket full of books made a third "reading center." On the wall above each of these centers, I posted a sentence strip. The line behind the tent read, "To the mountains . . ."; the one by the chair and rug read, "and back home." And the beach chair and towel sat beneath a sentence strip that read, "and to the ocean white with foam." The idea was that if reading takes you places, a book could take you to the mountains, the comfort of your own home, and even to the ocean.

On Open House night, I was especially anxious to see if my new students would like my room. I couldn't believe the reaction! First, a teacher came by and told me that in comparison to my classroom, his looked like a "hospital room." I walked to his room, and sure enough, I saw bare white walls staring at me. I offered him some of my leftover decorations and gave him some advice on making his own. Then, as I stood in my room to greet my students and their parents, I was amazed at how many people visited me. My classes weren't that big; I would be teaching only a small group of students per class, but I had hundreds of people walking through my room that night! Many said, "I heard about your room—I just came to see it."

On the first day of school, a student I didn't teach brought me a mobile made of starfish. "My mom saw your room," she said. "She wants you to hang this over at your ocean center." My own students loved the room, too. On the first day, they begged me to let them read in the tent. Keon said, "I don't even like to read, but if you let me get in that tent, I will. I'll read . . ."—he looked around at the buckets of books—". . . this book," he said. And he did!

Sadly, the fire marshal made me get rid of the tent just after school started, but now, years later, students still talk about it. Having that tent helped make my room just the adventure I wanted it to be.

Although I was proud of my classroom that year, and students really enjoyed being there, I have never been able to replicate the most amazing classroom I've ever seen, a third-grade class taught by my good buddy Alice. First of all, Alice had a beautiful glass-enclosed aviary in her room that sat at the children's eye level. The students were fascinated by the life cycle of the class mascots, Australian zebra goldfinches that had babies every nine weeks.

To the right of the birdcage sat another interesting addition to an elementary classroom: a porcelain clawfoot bathtub! There was an assortment of pillows in that tub, and kids clamored to get into it and read. Alice printed out a copy of Shel Silverstein's *There's Too Many Kids in This Tub* to decorate the reading area. To the right of the tub sat a real phone booth, just like the one Superman uses as a changing closet, another inviting place for kids to read. Clark Kent had left his glasses in that booth, and students could put them on, read a book, and become "Super Reader!"

Alice also had a loft, called Granny's Attic, where students could climb up and read with a life-size "Granny," a doll with posable arms that could wrap around children. Shelves under the loft held the only other tools needed for these engaging learning centers: books.

I look for that same type of engagement for my class and try to help students to feel "at home" at school, the same way I had felt on that first day in Mrs. Warnecke's room.

Making It About Them

Family is, of course, a good part of what makes a place feel like home. And it is apparent to me that students are more likely to be engaged in learning in a classroom when the room holds an atmosphere of family. Posting their baby pictures always enables us to feel close to each other, but last year I decided to try something new. I made silhouettes of each student employing the tried-and-true technique of elementary school teachers: using the overhead projector to cast a shadow of each student's profile on paper and tracing around it.

We began the year—literally on the first day of school—by writing our reading histories. I modeled the assignment, reading aloud what I had written about learning how to read in Mrs. Warnecke's classroom and continuing on to what I liked to read in high school and college and as an adult. My students wrote their histories, too, while one at a time, I called them over to the projector, pointed the light toward them, and outlined their profiles on black and brown paper. (I'd decided on a black-and-brown theme to contrast with the primary colors already so prominent in the room, another attempt on my part to be "artistic.")

After the students' reading histories were edited and typed, I hung them outside my classroom, each accompanied by its author's silhouette. The next day, it was like a carnival outside my room. The entire eighth grade stood outside my door and tried to figure out who was who by studying the silhouettes before reading the names on the histories. One pair of silhouettes stumped us all, me included: I had twin boys in my class that year, Jamal and Jalen. In fact, I think the boys themselves were unsure of who was who.

After the reading histories had been viewed for a while, I finally took them down and put them in writing folders, planning to deliver them back to my students. But I couldn't bring myself to file away the silhouettes. Instead I spread them out across a table in my room. There they were, all of my students—I wanted to keep them. So I borrowed the tallest ladder our custodian could find, and climbed to the ceiling to hang them on either side of the skylights. They stayed there all year, part of our classroom, and their human counterparts looked at and commented on them often.

All in a Nickname

One thing I have always loved as a teacher is calling the roll on the first day. This is kind of a crazy day because I don't know the students' names, and there is a great deal of room for error. And nothing is worse than mispronouncing a middle school student's name. Just ask my former student Chasskita. Her name is pronounced Chass-i-ka, but every teacher (including me) every year called her "Chass-kita" on the first day. And the look on her face by the time she got to me in seventh grade, having heard "Chass-kita" over and over, was painful to witness.

I used to unwittingly discover myriad opportunities for embarrassing students by calling attention to their names, usually through mispronunciation. Or, unbeknownst to me, the student would go by a middle name. Or the student would have a nickname I didn't know. So, thinking back to my college days, when professors called out last names with few mistakes, I figured this practice could work in a middle school classroom, too. Now I call out the student's last name, the surname—there are no nicknames for those—and instead of answering "Here" or "Present," the students respond with the name they wish to be called by.

Every year I get some interesting responses. One year a very small boy in the back of the room sat up tall when I called his last name, and responded, "My name is Snoop Doggy Dog!"

"OK, Snoop," I answered. "What does your mama call you?"

"Leroy," he whispered. Uh-huh, just as I thought. But for the rest of the year I called that little boy Snoop Puppy Pup—because he was way too small to be a dog. Sometimes I just called him Pup. He loved it.

Nicknames like this quickly become terms of endearment. One year when I was calling roll on the first day, a boy responded, "Anthony!" when I called out his last name. I looked up at him, and honestly, he was the cutest thing I'd ever seen. Without thinking I said, "Well, aren't you just cute as a bug?" The entire classroom fell into laughter, and I was afraid that I had embarrassed the boy. But he grinned, and several kids around him smacked him on the shoulder and called out, "Bug! Bug!"

It stuck. Bug was the boy's name from then on. Now Anthony is a grown man, but he still goes by Bug. And he'll always be Bug to me.

Having nicknames for students makes them feel special and loved, and it helps create the family atmosphere that I work to develop in the classroom. One year, I had a student named Crissy who would constantly brush her hair in class. I'd be teaching at the front of the room, and Crissy would spread her hair across the top of her desk and run her brush across it for as long as I would allow it. Of course, she soon became Prissy instead of Crissy. Nicole is Nick Nack Paddy Whack, Laura is Laura Lou, and Diana, a tiny little girl with a feisty attitude, is Pee Wee. Maurice became Peanut Head, and a beautiful girl named Diamond will always be Diamonds and Pearls. I still get e-mail from Juanesha, whose birth certificate says Juanita.

And I'm always thankful to the "grandmas" of our class. Every year I teach a girl who is the leader in the room, kind of the mama to the entire group. And every year I call that student Grandma. When I referred to the first student that way, years ago, I was concerned that it might sound negative, but I have found that those girls always like it! Chasskita was a grandma, a role she embraced with a smile.

> *Having nicknames for students makes them feel special and loved, and it helps create the family atmosphere that I work to develop in the classroom.*

Being a Little Crazy

Giving my students a nickname is a key to developing those all-important relationships in a classroom. But another thing I do is get crazy as often as I can. One of my goals is for there to be not one boring moment in my class.

> *I get crazy as often as I can. One of my goals is for there to be not one boring moment in my class. . . . Someone always announces, "She's gone crazy again!" But one thing is for sure: I have everyone's attention.*

For instance, I've never really given up my love for cheerleading, even after all these years of teaching. A correct answer is given or some appropriate behavior is achieved, and I'm kicking my leg up over my head. The first time I do it in front of a class, my students' mouths fall open in shock that this "old lady" can actually kick that high. After that, they beg for it, often trying to get their answers right so that I'll do the "cheerleader kick."

One time, when a student said two favorite middle school words that I hate, "I'm bored," I spun around, walked to the wall, turned back around, took a running start, and did a handspring in front of the class. Surprise can get a presenter a long way with an audience.

Dressing up can also command attention. I prefer to be a fairy. I've been a reading fairy, a testing fairy, and a focus fairy. I have wings, a boa, and a wand stashed in my cabinet, and when a student appears to be daydreaming, I'll say, "Oh . . . it's time for the Focus

Fairy!" I grab the ensemble, dance around the student's desk, and tap the wand all around while chanting, "Focus, focus, focus . . ."

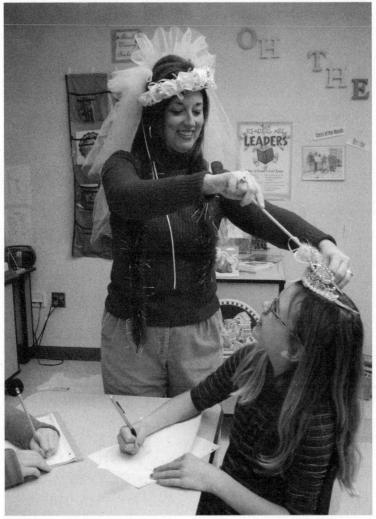

The Focus Fairy taps Savannah.

One year a teacher gave me a flyswatter for my classroom. This particular swatter is green with a big ornamental daisy affixed to one side. It has never been used to swat flies. Instead it is the "Focus Flower." When students engage in sidebar conversations while I'm teaching, I grab the Focus Flower and smack a desk, the board, a book, or a cabinet. All the students jump and then crack up laughing. Someone always announces, "She's gone crazy again!" But one thing is for sure: I have everyone's attention at that point.

Crazy voices can get similar results—as can singing (I can't carry a tune, unfortunately), dancing (those middle school dance moves are tough, let me tell you), and comic hysteria (volume is important for this one). It doesn't take too long until all eyes are on me. I've also been known to get a group focused by relating lessons to stories about my dog, illustrated with barking: those anecdotes snap students out of their daydreams pretty quickly.

These types of unexpected behavior can refocus students, but predictable classroom routines can also get the class to reconnect. For example, students love to repeat their favorite mantra: "That's not fair." I always respond, in the same exact words: "Fair is a weather condition and an event that comes to the county in the fall." After a couple of weeks, the students repeat it with me, and pretty soon, fairness is not a topic we discuss.

One classroom routine I love is the adoption of a class song. For the past few years, it's been "Unwritten," by Natasha Bedingfield. First, we listen to the song and read the lyrics together, and then we talk about the meaning. I ask my students to explain what it means to sing, "Today is where your book begins. The rest is still unwritten." Then I have them develop timelines of their lives. Students are accustomed to doing timelines. Many have done several in school along the way. But this timeline is different. It doesn't begin on the day they were born; instead, it begins on the day of the assignment and predicts the future. This assignment is meaning-ful, of course, but the best part is periodically playing the song while all of us dance around the room singing the lyrics. Only once have I been asked to "hold it down in there."

When I really get crazy, I throw things. Sometimes I just ran-domly throw candy. (I realize that candy, along

When I really get crazy, I throw things.

with the chicken biscuits I bring to class periodically and the pizzas I order, could be seen as contributing to adolescent—and teacher—obesity, but I think the dancing offsets it.) But my favorite things to throw are my "Smarty Beads." One year someone gave out strings of green beads, like Mardi Gras beads, as party favors. Because my school color is green, I took the necklaces to school and hung them around the classroom as decorations. Then, later that day, a student gave a spectacular answer—an answer that was so wonderful, I began looking around the room for something to serve as an award.

Suddenly I grabbed a necklace off the wall and said, "You get to wear the Smarty Beads!" Well, you'd have thought I said, *You get a million dollars!* After that, every student in the room wanted to wear the beads, and some students would come in from the halls and say, "Hey, can I get some of those beads?"

Generally the students return the beads at the end of class, and I hang them on a hook on the board, ready for the next class's correct answers. But occasionally, a student will acciden-tally wear them out of the room, and I've heard from other teachers that my Smarty Beads sometimes cause a stir in other classes. It seems students beg their friends to "share" as the beads get passed around the room. Once, after an accidental trip through the washing machine, a strand of green beads came back silver the next day. After that, all the students begged for the silver beads—until I went to a party store and bought all different colors. It was much preferable to give my students a choice than to hear them beg.

Getting a Clue

Color became a big part of my classroom magic in another way, too, and it happened somewhat by accident. Since my early days of teaching, and the lesson I learned when Curtis's father died, I've always been proud of my sensitivity to student problems. But just last year I needed a review of that lesson.

One day a student named Jamie came in agitated. I watched as he banged everything within reach on his desk—a pencil cup, a toy skateboard he grabbed from his pocket, and his binder, which he continued to open and close with a loud click. I couldn't get him focused; he refused to listen to me teach. Instead he was giggling and in constant motion, rocking back and forth in his chair for thirty straight minutes. I warned him repeatedly and used all of my strategies to redirect him. Finally, I mentioned my "last resort." I told him I was going to call his mother.

He jerked his head around and screeched at me, "SHE'S NOT THERE!!" I assumed he meant she was at work, so I called anyway. His dad answered and broke into my monologue: "I'm sorry to interrupt you, but you need to know: Jamie's mother left us last night."

I felt miserable, understanding now that Jamie's behavior made perfect sense. I think I'm pretty good, after all these years, at recognizing when something is troubling my students, but it can be difficult for a teacher to tell the difference between regular adolescent drama and life-changing traumas in a child's life. We are human, after all, and we can't read minds. So on that day, after my gaffe with Jamie, I came up with a plan that would change my classroom: mood cards.

I went to an office supply store and bought little metal cups—one for each desk in my classroom. The cups were designed to hold paper clips or thumbtacks, but in my room they hold mood cards. Each cup holds five different colored squares of construction paper, and each color represents a mood:

Red means *I'm angry, so leave me alone.*
Orange means *I'm annoyed or agitated.*
Blue means *I'm sad.*
Brown means *I'm bored.*
Green, the best card, means *I'm happy and having a great day!*

The students love these cards. If someone comes in distressed because of something that happened at home or in a previous class, we all know to leave that student alone for a while. Or on some days I'll look out and see a student with every single card spread across the desk. I'll say, "You can't be in *every* mood!"—but then I'll remember that we *are* talking about middle schoolers.

My students asked for two changes. First, they asked me to add a pink card to represent being in love, a request that I honored with a chuckle. My classes also asked me to put "the Teacher's Mood" on the board. So I made a little sign that reads "The

Teacher's Mood Is . . . ," and every day I place a green card on the board beside the sign. Sometimes, though, I'll play with the students: I walk over to the board and change the card to red. They say, "Ohhhh, she's mad now!" and I make my "mean face."

Once the mood cards were in place, something else happened that made a big difference in my classroom. Whenever students placed a red card on the desk, I asked if they wanted to talk about why they were mad. Now I realize that they almost always do. We began referring to these discussions as "issues," and our "Issues and Celebrations" time was born. I now begin every class period with Issues and Celebrations. I hear student issues about frustrations at home or in other classes, and I hear how many points my athletes scored the day before. This practice has become one of the highlights of my day—it enables me to really know my students and allows them to vent and celebrate in a safe atmosphere.

These discussions are one way that makes my classroom a place where students can learn. They know that I will do whatever it takes to make them successful. Not only do they know it: they can read it. Those very words—WHATEVER IT TAKES—hang on the front wall in letters five inches tall. I tell my students that I will do anything to help them be successful, even if I have to stand on my head. (Luckily, they haven't taken me up on that yet.) Beside those letters on the wall, I've placed a few more. I have a huge clipart picture of a finger pointing out at my classroom. Beside that picture are the words I BELIEVE IN YOU. And they know I do.

Somewhere along the way, I also started believing in myself as a teacher. Finally I was able to see in myself what Mrs. Warnecke had seen years before—potential. As I continue to touch the lives of children along the way, I continue to reach back in my memory to that first-grade year in an effort to be the teacher who makes a difference. I try everything I can think of—like the keys Mrs. Warnecke talks about—and I continue to do *whatever it takes* to be a good teacher, someone my first-grade teacher can be proud of.

❧ "Take a moment and catch your breath . . ."
—B. WARNECKE, APRIL 5, 2009

FIVE

Searching
for Strength

Teaching is hard. A teacher's daily life has more variables than almost any other profession. Anything from an announcement on the intercom to a student noticing one snowflake falling can turn a classroom upside down. Change the daily schedule for an assembly, and watch as normally compliant children become agitated and difficult to manage. Teachers leave school every day exhausted, most likely carrying work home with them—papers to grade and lessons to plan. So how do we find the energy to continue every day, to put one foot in front of the other and head back to that school building?

It's more difficult for beginning teachers because they haven't yet had a chance to see the differences they make with students. Many

You have to find your rewards in small pieces, in the day-to-day. . . . When Jose smiles for the first time because he's beginning to recognize words in English, when Tevin makes me a Valentine's card in art class, when Diana wraps herself around me when she enters my classroom, I seem to forget how tired I am.

times those messages come only years into a teaching career. So you have to find your rewards in small pieces, in the day-to-day. I believe that the more I give in the best interest of my students, the more I get back. When Jose smiles for the first time because he's beginning to recognize words in English, when Tevin makes me a Valentine's Day card in art class, when Diana wraps herself around me when she enters my classroom, I seem to forget how tired I am.

The year my father died, I received flowers and a huge platter of food from my students. I later learned that Therese had walked around the school building collecting money in a pickle jar. Meanwhile, Antonio, our class artist, painted me a watercolor picture titled "Saying Goodbye to Sadness." Kia came to the funeral home on her thirteenth birthday to see my family and to invite me to Denny's—to celebrate her special day. These are rewards that are difficult to find in any other profession, and they certainly offset the many nights that I have dragged myself home.

Whatever It Takes

There are teachers who believe you shouldn't take your work home, but I'm not one of them. I remember being accosted by one such colleague as I was walking to my car at the end of the day. She looked at my bag and said, "I used to do that too, but I stopped." For me, my classroom and my students are parts of who I am. I feel much more connected to my students on Monday when I have had their essays spread in front of me on Sunday afternoon. I've often told them that I feel as if I spent the weekend with them! And, like most teachers, I lie awake at night thinking of how to help a student with a particular concept, and all too often I toss and turn because of my concern over a student's circumstances. Although sometimes my worry may be more than is called for, other times it's barely enough.

Joey was a seventh grader who came to me in the middle of the school year. When he walked into my classroom that day, his bright smile held no suggestion of the difficulties he'd faced in his life. I soon learned that he had been taken from his mother by Social Services and had moved in with his aunt, who lived in our school district.

Just a week after joining my class, he was absent for several days—he was in the hospital. Concerned, I called to check on him and was told that his stomach was unable to handle the balanced meals of meat and vegetables that his aunt prepared for him; he was accustomed to eating mostly potato chips.

After Joey returned to school, I tried to make him feel a part of something new—to help him understand how important his education would be to his future. I also worked hard to catch Joey up on the work he had missed the first part of the year. He worked hard, too, but it was a major effort for both of us, because he hadn't learned the basics he needed to be successful in seventh grade. We worked together during my planning period and after school as often as he could get a ride home.

Joey soon adapted to the change in schools and made many friends. I can still picture him on the football field, where we would occasionally spend our recess time—he was always grinning out there and running like the free spirit he had not been allowed to be. But at other times it was apparent that he was focused on one thought: going home to his mother. He talked about it constantly, and I tried to help him understand that maybe he needed to be away from her for a while—so that they both could do better.

Joey was in my morning class, but one day he knocked on my door during my last class of the day. My first thought was that he had a question about homework. My students were working on a test, so I quietly walked over to the door.

"I came to tell you that I won't be here anymore after today," he said flatly.

"Joey, are you moving back with your mom?" I asked, trying to hide my concern.

"No," he said. And then, with no intonation in his voice, he added, "I'm going to kill myself when I get home."

I was immediately overcome with panic; my heart started pounding wildly. I had heard that when children are hysterical and melodramatic about suicide they are usually crying out for attention, and that although those students certainly deserve concern and care, those who are matter-of-fact and unemotional are the ones more likely to follow through on this type of threat. There was nothing hysterical about this child. He spoke of killing himself as if it were his only option. I glanced back at my class—they were quietly working—and then back at Joey, and tried to determine how to proceed. We didn't have phones in our rooms at that time, but the counselor's office was just across the hall, so I took Joey's arm and led him there.

After explaining to the counselor what had happened, I left Joey with her and returned to my classroom, still shaking.

Just as the dismissal bell rang, the counselor came to my door and told me that the school resource officer was taking Joey to the hospital. Without thinking, I blurted "I'm going with him!" and ran out the front door just as the officer's car was leaving the school lot. I jumped in my car, followed them to the emergency room, and was standing beside Joey's car door just as he stepped out. I told the officer that I would stay with him until his aunt arrived.

I walked with him to the intake nurse, and she began asking routine questions: "Do you have any allergies? Are you diabetic?"

Then, "Are you suicidal?"

Joey looked at me questioningly. I realized that he didn't know what the word meant.

"Joey," I said quietly, "she wants to know if you want to kill yourself."

He looked at her and answered as if it were the most normal response in the world, "Oh. Yeah."

The nurse jumped out of her seat and quickly escorted us to a "rubber room." I had heard of these types of rooms before, but I was unaware that they actually existed. The floor was made of a cushiony beige rubber, the walls were soft and rubbery, and the table and chairs were rubber and bolted to the floor. We sat there silent for several minutes. Then Joey spoke. "What are they going to do to me?" he asked.

"Joey, they're going to help you," I answered, my voice quivering.

Nothing in my teacher education program had prepared me for that moment, but I was sure I was where I needed to be.

Then I saw it. One tiny tear escaped from his eye and rolled down his cheek. Then another. That's all it took. He soon was weeping, and I was crying along with him. We sat on that spongy floor together, and I held him and rocked him back and forth while he cried for his mother. I remember thinking that nothing in my teacher education program had prepared me for that moment, but I was sure I was where I needed to be.

When Joey's aunt came, I slipped out to make arrangements for my own children to be picked up from school. When I returned, the hospital staff asked me to walk with Joey and his aunt to the psych ward. As we walked, they explained that he would be there for ten days, and there would be no communication with him; neither his family nor I would be allowed to speak with him until all the psychological assessments had been completed. It was one of the saddest experiences I had ever endured, walking down the dark, seemingly endless hall, through a series of doors that were unlocked and then shut clanging behind us, and finally leaving Joey there, alone, in that impenetrable place. I wept all the way home.

Ten days later, I was excited to see Joey outside, playing catch with some of his classmates before school. I asked him if he felt better. "A little taste," he said, as he told me about the antidepressant that was supposed to help him cope with the many changes in his life. He grinned his big toothy grin at me and threw a long pass to his friend, and I breathed for the first time in almost two weeks.

Joey returned to live with his mother before the end of the school year, and I lost touch with him, but never stopped thinking about what happened. As the years have gone by, I have shared this story with many others, and some have told me that accompanying Joey to the hospital was over and above what a teacher should have to do. But for me, it was life-changing: I became a better teacher because of that trip. Although I can't control what happens in a student's home life, that night I made a vow to give my students 100 percent every minute I have with them to try to keep them from feeling the despair that Joey felt. That night, on the spongy floor of that hospital room, the phrase Whatever It Takes was born. Once I made the commitment to embrace the word *teacher* at the core of who I am, I knew that I would work tirelessly to do what's best for kids. And that's what I strive for every single day I teach.

Ms. Dehart

I remember, as a child, sitting in my kindergarten classroom, excited as a learner, active, engaged, wanting to be like the teacher because she cared about us. This was my first inkling that I might want to be an educator. I went home and played school with my little chalkboard. I began to notice how the other students were catching on quickly to reading while I struggled to get a grasp on letter sounds.

I had trouble learning to read—first, second, third grade—I knew a few sight words, but I couldn't read. As the other children in my class whizzed through chapter books, I sat at my desk and cried. Teachers just dismissed me and worked with the others around me who were succeeding. It was devastating to be the only one the teacher overlooked.

Then, in fourth grade, I met Ms. Dehart. Ms. Dehart was like no other teacher I had ever met. She believed in me! For the first time in my young life, a teacher believed that I could learn to read. Ms. Dehart went the extra mile with me. We worked together for two months during the summer of my fourth-grade year. She pushed and pushed. Finally, after two months of working I read my first word, "chrysanthemum." As I read it, my eyes filled up with tears, and I knew that she was right—I could learn! I knew "if I can read 'chrysanthemum,' I can read anything!" What an "aha" moment that was, all made possible by the belief, faith, and effort of Ms. Dehart.

—Stephanie Doyle, sixth-grade history, James Breckinridge Middle
School, Roanoke, Virginia, 2009 Virginia Teacher of the Year

Giving the Time It Takes

One of the most important things I do is pledge to give my school, my classroom, and my students the time necessary to do my job well. I've attended Little League games, motorcycle races, and church services in an effort to support my students and their families. I have talked on the phone for hours with a student's parent going through a difficult divorce. And I always try to get to school as early as possible in the mornings. Getting to work a good twenty to thirty minutes before the official start time is necessary for me. It gives me time to think quietly about my day—and to make those all-important photocopies without waiting for someone else to finish.

After I've made my copies, written the day's agenda and goals on the board, and prepared the room, I have time for leisurely morning conversations with adults (there may not be another opportunity until after school) and for connecting with students as they begin arriving. Nothing is quite as meaningful as those early morning conversations when students hop off the bus to begin a new day.

Lest this all sound too goody-two-shoes, let me say that I do understand that there are sometimes *circumstances*. The year my son, Will, was a senior in high school, I skidded into the school parking lot on two wheels every morning just as the second hand on the office clock was announcing that I was late. If I didn't stay at home until he was safely belted into his car for the drive to school, he wouldn't get there. Not that he was a rebellious kid; he just kept falling asleep—in the bathtub, on the breakfast table. Basically any flat surface would do. (He just recently admitted that during his senior year he was always up half the night practicing his newly acquired skill of instant messaging—which, of course, led to morning naps in the bathtub.) So I do know that it can be difficult to get to the building early. However, I have found throughout my years of teaching that the earlier I can arrive at my school, the better the teaching day will be.

I feel the same way about the end of the school day. I once taught in a school that had what some of us referred to as the "3:30 Club." The club was made up of teachers who would walk to the bus parking lot (if they had bus duty) with their purses and book bags on their shoulders. I've never understood this. Looking at my colleagues standing in the parking lot ready to leave at 3:30, I would think about the classroom I had just left and the disarray I would encounter when I returned. How do those teachers pack up a room and feel prepared to leave the building so early? Hadn't students been in their care mere moments before?

It works better for me when I take my time in the afternoons, grade a few papers, look over some lesson plans, straighten up the room, and get it ready for the next day. Also, after school is a great time to catch up with colleagues. After all, aren't we the happiest in our jobs when we work among friends? You have to nurture those relationships. This part of the day is one of my favorites, standing around after school and catching up with other teachers. This is our time to share personal stories; it's the time we have a moment away from our students when we can discuss what's going on with our families, our children, and our interests outside of school. But most of all, I love to hear my colleagues' stories about what they have encountered during the day in a place where we may stand side by side for a few minutes at the copy machine or in the lunch line, but where we spend the majority of our time in our own classrooms with our students.

These interactions are important for other reasons as well. We teach the same kids. We're pursuing the same goals. It is absolutely necessary that we have time to share with each other. When I first began teaching, it was not uncommon for teachers to stay behind their closed doors with no opportunities for collaboration. But now we know that planning together improves instruction and having the support system of this type of professional learning community is imperative to our success. And these unplanned, spontaneous conversations that begin after school in the bus parking lot and car rider lane help make us more than colleagues. They make us friends.

I also like to wander around the school in the afternoons to see what my students are up to. There's nothing better than grading a few papers outside on the bleachers on a warm fall day during football season. My students, who should be paying attention to their coaches, always wave wildly when they see me in the stands, as if they didn't just see me in class thirty minutes before! I think it's good for both students and teachers to see each other outside the classroom now and then.

Not Giving Up

I do give a great deal of time and energy to my school and my students, but I'm not Wonder Woman. I'm human, and I have bad days like everyone else. One year I had a student who knew exactly what to say to get under my skin. He questioned the merit of every assignment and refused to do work. One day we were having one of our back-and-forth conversations, and I could feel the hair prickling on the back of my neck. Finally I said, "Corey, you really know how to push my buttons." Corey stood up beside his seat, gestured toward me, Supremes style (think: "Stop in the Name of Love"), and said in a slow drawl, "Puuussshhhhh." He repeated this move six times. After each "Push . . ." I quietly said his name, but I was getting more and more angry.

89

After the sixth repetition, Corey picked up a book off his desk and threw it in my direction. It landed three feet in front of me and slid across the floor as he continued saying "Puuussshhhhh." He threw each book on his desk in that way while I kept saying his name over and over, each time more loudly. The rest of the class watched, shocked at Corey's behavior, until finally I walked over, grabbed his arm, and escorted him to the office. I left him there and returned to my classroom, shaking with anger, to write the discipline referral.

The Whatever It Takes mandate stands, even when I have a conflict like that with a student. Because I have witnessed it on too many occasions, I know that some teachers would let the incident end there. But these types of confrontations keep me awake at night, tossing and turning in the effort to determine how I could have handled things differently.

> *I just cannot arrive at school and teach as if nothing has happened when I've had a difficult encounter with a student the day before.*

Many times I've called the student at home to work through the issue before we return the next day, but often the most troubled children don't have working telephones. I've resorted to e-mail and Facebook messages on occasion. Sometimes, though, it's just not possible to communicate with a student until the next day of school. And if there's a discipline referral involved, that student may be assigned to an in-school-suspension classroom. If that's the case, I head to that class as soon as school starts and ask to speak to the student. I just *cannot* arrive at school and teach as if nothing has happened when I've had such an encounter with a student the day before. It's a nonnegotiable for me: I must have a conversation with a student in this situation as soon as possible.

I've had many such conversations, and I can say with all sincerity that each time in my career that I've had a follow-up talk with a student after a conflict, I have walked away with a stronger bond with that child. The last time I lost my cool with a student was two years ago. The story is similar to the one with Corey: Brad refused to do work and disrupted the class constantly. After begging and pleading and being as nice as possible, I simply lost my patience one day and took him into the hall to have a "chat."

He got angry, the conversation escalated, and soon I was escorting him to the office. But I found him the next morning, after I had endured a sleepless night replaying the scene in my head, and we worked through our conflict. Brad didn't change overnight, though; teachers still struggled with his behavior on a daily basis. So a few months later, he was sent to our school district's alternative school. That spring, however, when our students from that school were brought back for standardized testing, Brad told the administrator that he refused to take the test unless he could take it with me. He recognized the extra effort that I had put into working with him, and it had enabled us to establish a connection that he hadn't found elsewhere.

Who Was It Today?

When I was a novice teacher, I began practicing a reflection activity that I called "Who was it today?" When I was struggling, and wondered if I was making a difference as a teacher, I would take a moment to sit down after school every day and ask myself whether I had made an impact on at least one child during the course of the day.

Sometimes, in those early days, the answer to the question was often seemingly insignificant—something as small as a student smiling at me because I complimented her on her new shoes. But, still, it gave me something to hold on to when I wasn't sure I was making a difference.

Later I heard the story of the star thrower, based on an essay by anthropologist and author Loren Eiseley, which tells of a little girl picking up starfish on the shore and throwing them back into the ocean. A man approaches the child to tell her that what she was doing was futile; there are too many beached starfish. The little girl picks up another starfish, throws it into the ocean, and says, "That's one."

For years, I adopted the "that's one" philosophy of teaching. After all, I was "one" who had benefited from the tireless effort of a teacher—surely I could be that same type of teacher. That knowledge validated my early days, but as a veteran teacher I now realize that "one" is not enough. I have to reach all of them. I must be sure that each and every child is a starfish that is tossed back. And it's only through practicing genuine care and concern and giving extra hours to my job that I have a chance to make a difference to them all.

I myself was that starfish once, and throughout my teaching years there would be reminders time and time again. Once I walked into my school's teacher workroom and saw these words from John Steinbeck on a poster:

> In her classroom, our speculations ranged the whole world.
> When she left we were sad, but her light did not go out. She

had written her indelible signature on our minds. I suppose, to a large extent, I am the unfinished manuscript of such a person. What awesome power lies in the hands of such a person.

I read it aloud and then whispered, tears in my eyes, "Mrs. Warnecke."

I remain, I hope, her unfinished manuscript, and to this day, I work to do whatever it takes to live up to that challenge.

* "A dream only remains a dream if you
don't have the courage to try."
—B. WARNECKE, MAY 24, 2009

SIX

Bringing Dreams to Light

Classroom teachers are painfully aware of interruptions in the classroom. I'm not talking about student disruptions; instead I'm referring to the intercom, student messengers running errands for the office, and colleagues who stop by to ask "vital" questions about the textbook selection process while you're trying to deliver a compelling lesson. These distractions are common in schools and an inevitable part of the work day—you pause to take care of whatever it is, and move on.

But sometimes the seemingly mundane turns out to have broad repercussions. For instance, a classroom interruption that occurred in my fifth year of teaching changed my first days of school for the remainder of my career. I had just assigned a short reading passage and was standing, as it happened, close to the classroom door as my students worked on the assignment. Hearing a light tap on the door, I opened it to see a petite eighth-grade girl standing there. I expected her to be carrying a note from a colleague, but instead she cheerfully announced that she was a reporter for the student newspaper and wanted to interview me. I agreed and asked her to come back after school.

Later that day we sat down at a couple of student desks, and she uncapped her pen. Her first question was, "Why do you teach?"

I was stuck for an answer. I had spent five years trying to figure out *how*—I hadn't thought about *why*. Without thinking, I gestured out across the room and said, "Do you know who sits at these desks?" She looked confused, so I continued. "People's children. These are people's dreams come true. Someone wanted these children their whole lives, and it's a great honor to teach someone's dream. That's why I teach."

As the student reporter wrote down my words on her pad, I looked down and whispered under my breath, "That may be the cheesiest thing I've ever said." But that night and over the days and weeks that followed, I thought about my answer, and it started to seem less embarrassing. Maybe I had been on to something.

Opening a Window to the Future

When school began the next year, I delivered my "First Day of School Motivational Dream Speech" for the first time.

I have often noticed that the first day is the best time to say something really important, something that you really want students to hear. Our kids are usually a little timid on that day, still trying to figure out the teacher and their classmates. (The first day is also the best day because, unlike any other day of the year, the students have *school supplies*! Yes, they have a binder, they have loose-leaf paper, and they have ninety-two pencils. How many pencils do they have the second day? Zero. Where do they go? I often picture them as projectiles flying out of school bus windows across rural roads and city streets . . . farm animals and house pets running for their lives!)

So the first day is the day I deliver my First Day of School Motivational Dream Speech, while many teachers up and down the hallway are explaining the classroom rules and procedures. As soon as the students are settled and I've finished calling the roll (by last name), I pause for a moment and look across the class. Then I throw the question out at them: "How many of you have ever thought about the kids you'll have someday?"

Of course, they are immediately thrown off guard, and I get some puzzled looks. I can almost read their minds: *I thought this was language arts* and *I bet she's gonna make us write something*. But I always get the girls' attention at that moment, and slowly the hands begin rising across the room. I continue with, "How many of you have already named your babies?" Now the girls can't wait to tell me their babies' names, and I usually have a couple of boys who'll add to the discussion by announcing, "I'm going to name my baby Junior!"

We continue for a few minutes discussing baby names. Over the years I have learned that middle school girls have named all their babies—with first, middle, and last names—and that the last names are different from their own (commonly they have the last name of some current pop star).

After the name discussion, I ask my next question: "Do you realize, that when your parents were in seventh grade, they sat in desks just like these and thought about you? Do you know what that makes you?" At this point, they look really puzzled, so I tell them, "That makes you someone's dream come true. And as someone's dream come true, you have a lot to live up to."

Now the room is totally silent. Students are thinking through all of this and likely wondering where I'm going with it. In all the silence, usually some boy from the back of the room will break the silence with a thought: "Dude! My parents were in seventh grade?!"

I use the rest of the class period, that entire first day of school, to talk with my students about dreams. I tell them that we're going to spend the year discussing our own aspirations and dreams, the characters' dreams in the books that we read throughout the year, and Dr. Martin Luther King Jr.'s dreams as outlined in his immortal "I Have a Dream" speech. I ask my students, "If Dr. King came back today, would he say his dream has been realized?" They always agree that he would say we've come a long way, but have a long way to go.

I also share that during the school year we will write our own "I Have a Dream" speeches. Students are always excited about this possibility, and I get various renditions involving dreams of becoming professional athletes and hip-hop artists. But my favorite student speech was written by Kyle, a twelve-year-old, who wrote, "I have a dream that Courtney will go out with me. I asked her once, but she said 'No.' I'll ask her again . . . when I'm her height."

During our discussion of dreams that first day, after I explain the responsibility of being someone's dream come true, I tell them that teachers have dreams, too. The students all want to hear what mine is, so I tell them: "It is my dream to be what I refer to as 'the one.' I want to be the one that my students look back on one day and say, 'She was the one who taught me such-and-such. She was the one who cared. She was the one who made a difference.'"

One year I saw two of my students shoving each other in the lunch line on the first day of school. I quietly walked over and said, "You're stepping on my dream. I can't be 'the one' if you're not doing what you're supposed to be doing." One of the boys playfully smacked the other on the shoulder and declared, "Man! Don't step on her dream!" Those two boys were the first to dub me "the Dream Teacher," a name that stuck that year and has followed me throughout my career.

One year I was delivering my speech when I noticed Robin, a student who happened to be sitting right in front of me that day, looking skeptical. I didn't say anything at that moment; instead I waited to get to know more about my new student and her frustrations. I soon found out that her mother had died a few years before when Robin was in elementary school. She was much too sad to have room for dreams.

But that year I tried to help her understand how to get her sadness out of inside herself and onto paper instead. She wrote poems, she wrote stories, and she wrote letters to her mother. At the end of the year, she wrote a poem for me. I've carried it from classroom to classroom for many years, and now I keep it in my teacher bag so that I can share it with other teachers. I don't have to look at it to remember one stanza that is so meaningful to me:

I'm trying to say thanks
It meant so much
That my heart got picked
For you to touch.

Years after that student reporter asked me, I finally knew the real answer to why I teach.

Mr. Caviness

All of us can reflect upon our educational journeys and remember the teachers who had an impact on our lives. I am indebted to the numerous teachers who have shaped me as an individual. The teacher who influenced me the most was my high school chemistry teacher. I dreaded taking his class because chemistry concepts were difficult for me to understand. However, Elton Caviness was determined to make his students enjoy this subject area with his unique sense of humor and caring personality. He never minded getting distracted to share jokes or to provide life lessons when needed. He was the star actor in school plays, the announcer at the basketball games, and the club adviser for Quiz Bowl. He stayed involved with these important activities to support his students and the school. Mr. Caviness ensured a positive learning environment by earning respect from his students instead of constantly demanding it. Students would choose to eat lunch in his classroom just to be in his company. I can also remember laughing with classmates when we would see how much chalk dust would cover Mr. Caviness's shirt and tie because he would get so excited about explaining a new concept on the chalkboard. He worked diligently to make learning meaningful and memorable. For example, so that we could understand the process of chemical reactions, we made homemade ice cream in class. Each time I eat homemade ice cream, I think about Mr. Caviness's project.

It is undeniable that Mr. Caviness was a leader in the school and community with his desire to make a difference in the lives of others. He encouraged all of us to select a career pathway in life and to never look back. Because of Mr. Caviness, I now stand in front of my own students hoping to inspire them in the same way—to achieve their dreams. And incidentally, I am even more proud to call Mr. Caviness my father.

—Trisha Muse, fourth-grade teacher, Page Street Elementary School, Troy, North Carolina, 2008–2009 North Carolina Sandhills/South Central Regional Teacher of the Year

Learning from Dreams

Another year, when I was talking about dreams, a student named Eddie raised his hand and asked, "What happens if somebody stomps on your dream and smashes it all to bits?"

Thinking back many years to the demise of my cheerleader dream, I answered, "Well, Eddie, you basically have two choices. You can scrape your dream up off the pavement and go after it again. Or you can get a new dream and go after that one as hard as you can."

Eddie had decided that he wanted to be a wrestler for the middle school wrestling team. He was not the biggest kid in seventh grade, but boy did he go after his dream that year! He worked nonstop at wrestling. He wrote about it in his journals, he

I finally knew the real answer to why I teach.

talked about it constantly, and gradually he grew to be really good at it. By the end of the season, he was undefeated, and the other students had begun calling him "Bubba." It was great to go to the wrestling matches and hear the fans chanting, "Bub-ba, Bub-ba, Bub-ba . . ."

Eddie eventually won the state championship in his weight class in high school—he was a talented wrestler—but as a seventh grader, he was mostly just *wiggly*. He had a big personality and was extremely bright, but many teachers categorized Eddie as somewhat of a class clown: one joke and he could distract an entire roomful of seventh graders. I loved him, though, and I was proud of his work ethic as he went after his athletic goals.

Over the winter break that year, when teachers and students were home for that much-needed two-week rest, one night I dreamed—or really, *nightmared*—about my students. I dreamed that we were returning from a field trip, with the entire seventh grade piled into three chartered buses. I was on the first bus to arrive back on campus. We pulled up to the curb, and the students and I filed off the bus. Then we stood and waited for the second bus to arrive. The second group of students hopped off the bus, and, in my dream, we all turned to look toward the third bus as it approached.

At that moment, the third bus exploded right before our eyes. We screamed in terror, and then we were all crying, students and teachers alike, for the dear friends we had lost on that bus. Students came running to me, yelling, "Who was on that bus?"

I read the list aloud to the students: "Crystal Blalock," I said, and everyone gasped.

"Oh, I loved her," I mourned.

"Anthony Barger." Another gasp. By now we were all crying and hugging. I read the next name: "Eddie Bubba Haywood." The cries became sobs.

"Not Eddie!" we all screamed. "We love him. He's such a talented wrestler. What a great guy!"

At that moment, in my dream, I felt a tug on my sleeve. I looked around, and there stood Eddie. Bubba himself was standing there grinning at me the way he always did from his seat in the back of my classroom.

"Eddie!" I screamed. "What are you doing here? You're listed on bus number 3, and we just watched it blow up!"

Eddie, still grinning, scuffed the ground with his wrestling shoe. "Yeah . . . uh . . . I was on the wrong bus."

Silence. Shock. Incredulous stares from the rest of the students. Then, "Of course you were!" I yelled. "You're always in the wrong place, Eddie Haywood! What were you thinking?"

I woke up then. I had really been crying in my sleep—my pillow was soaked. I was crying for Crystal, for Anthony, for Bubba Haywood, my dream students who I thought were gone. It was 4 AM, but I wanted to call all my students right then and tell them how much they meant to me. I was thinking that if anything should ever happen to them, I would want them to know how I felt about them. I restrained myself, however.

A week later, school started again. The first day back after a break is always an important one in a school. As on the first day of school in the fall, everyone is fresh and rested, and it tends to be a somewhat quiet day. I always use the first day back to revisit classroom procedures, implement new classroom management plans, and discuss goals for the remainder of the school year. But this particular day, I chose to tell my students how important they were to me.

I began by reminding them of my original dream speech at the beginning of the year. Some of them laughed quietly: "Here she goes again." I then told them that sometimes our nighttime dreams overlap with our lives. I told them about my dream over break, about the lost students on the blown-up bus, and last, about Eddie, the almost-lost student who had been on the wrong bus. Telling this story was definitely a highlight of that year. Not only did they enjoy the story and hearing their own names in it (I had a long list of "lost" students by the time I told the story), but they thought the part about Eddie was hysterical. Because they all knew him and knew his personality, they thought the fact that he had messed up again and was on the wrong bus was particularly funny. They began chanting right there in the classroom: "Bub-ba . . . Bub-ba . . . Bub-ba . . ." while Eddie sat in his back-row desk and grinned.

The dream, I told them, had special meaning to me. I didn't ever want to repeat the feeling that I had that morning upon waking and thinking that something had happened to my students, especially wondering if they didn't understand how important they were to me. So I used this chance to tell them simply, "I love you guys!" They laughed like I was crazy and told me that they loved me, too. I promise you that after a class period like that, it's a great deal easier to teach pronouns the next day.

Although that was when the "Dream Teacher" was born, those dreams of mine had begun decades before, in a first-grade classroom in 1963, the same year Dr. Martin Luther King Jr. shared his own dream with the world. Because I had a giving teacher who was open about how she felt about her students, I was able to look back years later, pull from that experience, and offer my own students the same devotion.

Waking up in tears that morning had the effect of reminding me vividly of that young teacher. I began to realize how badly I wanted to tell her about my dreams of being a teacher who makes a difference. I wanted her to know that she was that teacher for me. But I had lost her back in 1967 when she moved away. Forty years is a long time, and I had no idea where she might be. Still, I had a dream that one day I would find her and tell her my story. And, of course, dreams sometimes can come true.

"Of course I remember you . . ."

—B. WARNECKE, SEPTEMBER 5, 2008

SEVEN

Finding Mrs. Warnecke

Over the years, I often thought about my first-grade teacher and wondered if she remembered a little girl with skinny legs from a damp basement classroom. As a student, I would compare my other teachers to her: if they were kind and inspirational, I would think of Mrs. Warnecke's similar qualities; if they were impatient or critical, I would silently wish they were more like her.

Once I decided that I would major in education, I envisioned a conversation with my Mrs. Teacher, one that would allow her to give me all the advice I needed to be successful in my own future classrooms. As a struggling teacher, I often thought back to my first-grade year and wondered what I needed to do to ensure that some student, *any* student, would think of me years later, as I was thinking of Mrs. Warnecke.

In 2008, an amazing thing happened to me: I was named the Teacher of the Year for North Carolina. I felt undeserving, but honored and humbled, as I thought back over my career and my rocky beginnings. It was that year that I began to really reflect on my life—my life as a student and then as a teacher—and I wanted Mrs. Warnecke to know that I had worked for over twenty years to emulate her.

It's not surprising that I would have these thoughts at this time. As part of my Teacher of the Year duties, I was pulled from the classroom to serve as my state's "Teacher Ambassador," and I put thousands of miles on my car as I traveled around speaking on behalf of teachers and education, encouraging high school and college students to consider teaching as a profession, and trying to inspire new teachers to continue to work toward making a difference in children's lives. I heard similar questions everywhere I went: Who inspired you as a teacher? Why do you think you were selected your state's Teacher of the Year? I found myself describing Mrs. Warnecke's teaching expertise and unconditional expression of kindness in so many of my answers that she was much on my mind during this time.

TV News Connections

Generally, when I'm getting ready for work, I have the television on in the background, tuned to the local morning news, which is on right before ABC's *Good Morning America*, and I end up catching part of the latter show as well. I'd been a fan of *GMA* for years, especially since the time Charles Gibson and Diane Sawyer had visited the University of North Carolina campus a few years before. My daughter, Kelli, had been a cheerleader at UNC then, and I'd made up a cheer for her squad to perform that included the names of the *GMA* anchors. I was on the campus that day, snapping pictures like an annoying cheerleader mom while I watched Kelli living my dream of being a college cheerleader. And I watched as Mr. Gibson and Ms. Sawyer joked with the excited crowd of college students, laughed at the lyrics of my homemade cheer, and nuzzled the mascot, a ram with blue horns named Ramses.

A few years after that I'd sent anchor Robin Roberts a card when I was moved by her on-air breast cancer announcement. My own mother is a breast cancer survivor, and I lost my dad to bone marrow cancer the same year Ms. Roberts's father died. I was excited, but not surprised, when I received a letter in reply to my card. The entire *GMA* cast and crew seem to be extensions of our own families, neighbors from hundreds of miles away who sit in our dens every morning and chat with us.

The day I was preparing to speak to teacher education majors at Duke University began the same as most other days: I was applying makeup while my friends in New York chatted about current events, though I wasn't paying much attention to the show; I was thinking about my presentation. Then I realized something special was happening on *GMA*. I looked over at the television to see a young woman from Nebraska sharing the details of a near-drowning experience that had occurred when she was a child. On the show that day, she would finally be able to thank the man who saved her by pulling her from a lake one afternoon thirty years before.

I watched, spellbound, as the woman recounted the events and then thanked the man who had saved her life. She presented him with a scrapbook—a testament to the years she had experienced as a result of a stranger's kindness. I stood there, tears ruining my just-applied makeup, and listened as morning anchor Chris Cuomo ended the segment with this statement: "If you'd like to thank someone who's made a difference in your life, go to the *Good Morning America* Web site."

I stood there in my bedroom, looked at Chris Cuomo on my television, and blubbered through tears, "*I wanna thank Mrs. Warnecke.*" Then I washed my face, reapplied my makeup, and went to work with a renewed mission of enabling future teachers to understand the importance of their jobs.

I was so occupied with my teaching and "ambassadorial" duties that I forgot for a few weeks to write to *GMA* about my desire to thank Mrs. Warnecke. One night my husband, David, and I were playing TV tag—you know, the game where he, holding the remote control, tunes into a show for twenty seconds or so, just long enough for me to get interested, and then—click—moves on to the next one. Again. And again. I finally looked at him and yelled, "STOP IT!" He then turned the remote toward me and pressed the Mute button.

In protest, I got up and went to the dining room to pick up my laptop, planning to pass the time perusing some education Web sites instead of playing tag with my husband. Once I had the computer in my lap, I thought, *Hey, what about that* Good Morning America *thank-you thing?* and immediately clicked on the Web site. There it was, a simple little box beckoning to me, a place for me to share the secrets of my childhood. I began typing, and I didn't stop until it was all there: Mrs. Riley, Sheila, my skinny legs and unruly hair, the basement, Mrs. Warnecke, the poetry I wrote for her . . . everything. I clicked Submit and didn't think about it again.

A Journey into the Past

Then, a month later, late in the evening, I received an e-mail from Brian O'Keefe, a *GMA* producer: "Hi Cindi, I'm a producer for Good Morning America, and we like your story about your teacher Barbara. Can I call you?"

My first thought was, *Who's Barbara?*—to me she will always be "Mrs. Warnecke" or "Mrs. Teacher," not *Barbara*. My second thought was, *What kid has hacked into the GMA Web site and stolen my information?!* I couldn't believe that anyone would be interested in my story. But I replied with my phone number—my *cell* phone number, not my home number, lest he be a stalker or a pervert!—and waited. My phone rang a minute later, at 11:30 PM.

"Cindi, this is Brian. I'm sorry about the time difference. I'm in L.A." My heart started pounding wildly. L.A.? As in *Los Angeles?!*

Brian told me that he and the other *GMA* producers had enjoyed my story about my long-lost teacher. He went on to tell me that the *GMA* staff had been searching for Mrs. Warnecke but hadn't found her. He asked me for any information I had on her: her last known address, her husband's name. I answered as best I could. But I felt so limited. I was talking about someone I hadn't heard from since 1970, the last time I received a letter from Mrs. Warnecke.

Brian did surprise me by saying, "We haven't found her, but we know she's not dead. Death records are easy to obtain. So she's out there somewhere."

And although this announcement was a relief, I still felt a flurry of emotion as Brian told me that he would continue to look for Mrs. Warnecke and that he wanted to fly me to New York to be on the show. He promised to stay in touch, and I went to bed that night trying to visualize what my first-grade teacher might look like.

Mrs. Warnecke has always been a mythological being to me, the perfect teacher of my memories, a perpetually smiling and caring young lady. I tried to envision her as an older woman and thought that maybe she would be my mother's age, in her eighties. I pictured a *GMA* reunion and wondered if she would hobble in behind her walker or lean on a cane. I then pictured her in a wheelchair with an accompanying oxygen tank. What if she was, indeed, *feeble?* Would this version of Mrs. Warnecke quickly erase the heroine of my memory? And what if I never found her? What if I appeared on national television and made a plea to find someone who didn't want to be found? Surely Mrs. Warnecke would be living a happy, peaceful, most likely *private* life somewhere and wouldn't want it disrupted by a student from long ago whom she didn't even remember.

A few days later, Brian called again to say that I would be appearing on *Good Morning America* in a Back to School special. On the show scheduled to air September 5, 2008, the day after my fifty-first birthday, I would tell the world my story. We would all hope that Mrs. Warnecke or someone who knew her would be watching. I rushed to the bookstore to purchase a copy of *You Read to Me, I'll Read to You,* the same book Mrs. Warnecke had given me forty years before. I wanted to have it with me in the event that, miraculously, Brian was able to find her. I inscribed it, thanking Mrs. Teacher for making a difference in my life, and tucked it away just in case.

A week before my trip to New York, Brian and his crew pulled up in front of my house to interview me, my mother, my sister, and my daughter about Mrs. Warnecke and about me as a teacher. As they unloaded equipment and set up lights, cameras, and screens, my neighbor came over and asked me, "What'cha doin'? Making a movie?" I did feel like a movie star for one second as that camera started rolling. But somewhere along the way, my conversations about Mrs. Warnecke transformed me back to little Cindy Cole, an insecure first grader. It didn't take long during the interview for the tears to come. Brian asked me if thinking about finding Mrs. Warnecke was emotional for me, and what I would want to say to her if I had the chance.

I answered, as a tear rolled down my cheek, "It *is* very emotional. I want her to know that there was a skinny little girl once who didn't feel good about herself. And then one day everything changed. And because of that day my life turned out differently, and, hopefully, because of that, there are many students that I've had an impact on, and their lives turned out differently, too."

The emotional journey into the past continued later that afternoon, as Brian and I drove the few miles to the site of my former elementary school. Bragtown School, that building that had housed that meaningful first-grade experience, had burned to the ground in 1991. I was teaching a few miles away then, at a nearby middle school, and I stood on the football field watching the billowing smoke rise above the trees, weeping along with many of my colleagues as we watched a piece of our history being destroyed—several of the other teachers had taught there just the year before. That old building, built in 1927 with beautiful hardwood floors gleaming with over sixty years of waxing, didn't stand a chance against such a raging fire. In less than an hour, the school and my chance of ever seeing my basement classroom again were gone.

So on this day, I walked Brian around the grounds, saying, "This is where the playground was" and "The gym would have been right here." I longed to be able to actually *see* my old school, to touch a brick, to sit in that cafeteria one more time and eat homemade vegetable soup and a yeast roll. But it would never be. I would have to settle for my memories, some crisp and clear, others faded and dim. That realization made my trip to the site even more emotional.

Mrs. Burnett

"Is this my little Susie?" asked the voice on the phone.

"Yes, ma'am," I responded.

It was Mrs. Burnett, my sixth-grade language arts and history teacher. She was the teacher who made a difference. She was the one who inspired me to teach.

Mrs. Burnett wore beautiful clothes and expensive shoes that came from Leon's, the best shop in town. Although she was a tiny woman, students quaked when she gave them her teacher look over the top of her half glasses. We wrote reports on mythology, important historical sites, and the Seven Wonders of the World. My first experience with research began with my World Book Encyclopedias. I was supposed to write about the Acropolis. I began at "aardvark" and worked my way back. Knowing just to know was fun.

Each week Mrs. Burnett gave us cumulative vocabulary tests—no true-false or matching, and by the time we finished the last four-hundred-word test, I had fallen in love with words. When I received the Agnes Meyer Distinguished Educator Award from *The Washington Post*, I wrote Mrs. Burnett. I wanted to let her know that I had done well following her example. She wrote me back telling me that she was proud of me. It mattered a lot.

It had been almost ten years since we exchanged letters, and I was a little surprised, but glad to discover that at age ninety-eight, Mrs. Burnett would be a guest of honor at our fortieth class reunion. I couldn't get back to Texas to attend, so wrote her again recalling the poetry we'd learned, the vocabulary words and the history notebook she had us keep. I wanted to tell her again that she had made a difference, that I had written about her, and that I had managed to grow up to be like her—a teacher who taught her students not just to know, but to think.

And now, here she was, almost fifty years later, on the phone:

"So you are writing now! I always knew you had great potential, Susie. You know, teachers aren't supposed to feel this way, but

you're a teacher too, so you understand that no matter careful we are to be fair, we can't help but feel closer to some students. You were always my favorite."

"You were my favorite too, Mrs. Burnett. You taught me how to be a teacher."

I wonder if I'll ever get to make the same kind of call.

—Susan Graham, family and consumer science teacher, Gayle Middle School, Fredericksburg, Virginia, 2000 Virginia Region III Teacher of the Year

In the Spotlight

The next week, my husband and I flew to New York. I don't believe I've ever been so nervous in my entire life. I slept very little the night before the show, trying to organize my words so that they would make sense on national television. Many people talk about teachers who've made a difference. How could I explain to the world the impact that Mrs. Warnecke had on me? How would I be able to describe the insecurities I had as a first grader and the way that one day, the day that I was placed in a new first-grade classroom, seemingly changed the entire direction of my life?

The morning of September 5, David and I arrived at the *GMA* studios early, before 6:30 AM. We met Katie, one of the producers, at the door, and she walked us to the dressing room. Katie, along with several crew members along the way, lamented that it would have been "really cool" if Mrs. Warnecke had been found instead of my having to make a plea on national television for someone else to find her. So many people said those very words to me that by the time I arrived at my dressing room, I was sure that she wasn't there, that there would be no surprise reunion. I decided to savor the moment anyway, though, because I knew my students would be watching at school, and they would want to see pictures and hear all about the experience later. So David photographed everything from my getting my makeup applied by a professional to my standing terrified in the studio waiting to go on.

After my hair and makeup were done, I sat in my dressing room and tried to compose myself. I thought of Mrs. Warnecke and how I would feel myself if I someday turned on the television to see one of my former students talking about me. Katie sat there with me, making small talk about teachers she remembered. After she left to check on the time with the other producers, I tried to listen to some music, but I was too wound up. I jumped a foot when Katie came back to say it was time to go to the studio.

We walked past Robin Roberts's dressing room—appropriately labeled with a sign that read "Robin's Nest." She and Diane Sawyer were at the Republican National Convention that day, so I wouldn't have the chance to meet them. But that was OK—I was too nervous to think about that missed opportunity. After a ride on an elevator big enough to hold a pickup truck, we stepped into the studio. Although I'd seen it on my television for years, it looked entirely different from that perspective. The first thing I noticed was that it was very crowded: there was the studio audience and tons of crew members working cameras and carrying cords. I'd never seen this organized chaos on my morning television. Once I got my bearings,

Waiting for my television debut. My teeth were chattering, but I was trying to smile.

I saw the smiling face of the weatherman, Sam Champion, who reached out and shook my hand as though we were old friends. I then saw famous TV chef Sarah Moulton, who had prepared back-to-school snacks, in keeping with the day's theme.

Katie told me to stand behind a camera to wait, and I did, frozen in terror. David continued to take pictures of me, but I was too scared to smile, instead clenching my teeth in an effort to keep them from chattering. Part of me was scared that they, in fact, *had* found my first-grade teacher and that she would have no recollection of me. I wondered what I could say to jog her memory. And if she did recall a sad little first grader, how would I find words to help her understand her mythological status in my mind for over forty years?

But there was little time to mull over those worries. I heard Chris Cuomo go to a commercial, and before I knew it, Katie was guiding me to a chair. I sat there momentarily, after a warm greeting from Mr. Cuomo, and then I heard the countdown to air: 5, 4, 3, 2 . . .

Immediately I was in elementary school again—all of us are sitting on the floor around a television set that has been brought in for that day only. We're watching one of the Apollo rockets blasting off, and we are chanting together to liftoff: 5, 4, 3, 2 . . .

Then I heard Chris Cuomo's voice: "And this morning we have a back-to-school theme and one woman's plea to find her first-grade teacher who forever changed her life . . ." I tried to breathe, and I looked at the video that was playing on the monitor in front of me. There, in all its glory, was Bragtown School, a black-and-white version of the schoolhouse of my childhood. I could smell the floor wax and the musty gym, and I could hear the librarian, Mrs. Chandler, telling us the Br'er Rabbit stories and Mrs. Veasey, the bus driver for bus number 58, telling us to sit down in our seats. I felt the hard binding of a *Dick and Jane* book, while Mrs. Warnecke read aloud in front of the class.

I came back to the present when I saw my sister on the monitor, talking about my insecurities, and I wondered if I'd made the right decision to put my life out there for the entire country to see. Next I saw my eighty-year-old mother, who at that moment was five hundred miles away in North Carolina, on screen talking about Mrs. Warnecke and me. I looked at Mr. Cuomo and mumbled, "That's my mama . . ." and thought for sure that I would burst into tears.

Then I saw myself—on the monitor—crying while answering questions about my teacher's impact on my life. Meanwhile, the me in the studio was just trying to breathe and talking furiously (if silently) to myself: *Just hold it together. The whole country is already seeing your first- and second-grade pictures. Don't embarrass yourself even more by weeping on camera!*

Finally the clip of my school and my childhood ended. Mr. Cuomo then asked me why it was so important for me to find my teacher. Luckily, the answer to that was the one I'd been formulating since 3 AM. I told him that everyone has a Mrs. Warnecke, that we all have teachers who make an impact on us, but that many times the teachers never find out that they've made a difference. I then told him that I wanted Mrs. Warnecke to know that "she was that person for me."

Chris Cuomo then told me that *GMA* had conducted an investigation and had found someone who could help me find my teacher. I sat for a moment, thinking, *If you've found someone who can help find her, why didn't you just get that person to find her and then bring her here?!* Then I heard cheering and clapping—I was already crying when I looked at Chris Cuomo and said, pleadingly, "Did you find her?"

Finally Found

And then I saw her. Mrs. Warnecke. My Mrs. Warnecke. She looked the very same! She wasn't a little old lady with a walker; she wasn't even old (in fact, she looked my age!). Same face, same smile, same loving and caring demeanor. My hands flew to my face. I kept repeating, "Oh, my gosh . . . oh, my gosh . . ." while hugging Mrs. Warnecke and crying.

My first words to her were to ask her if she was mad that I brought her on national television. She replied that she was honored. Then I asked her if she remembered me.

"Of course I do!" she answered, and we walked over to join Chris Cuomo in the guest chairs.

I absolutely could not believe that I was sitting beside Mrs. Warnecke! Twice I reached over and touched her on the arm—I think I was trying to determine if she was real and not one of my lifelong memories.

During the interview, I found out that when Brian, the producer, called Mrs. Warnecke and told her that a former student was looking for her, she replied, "Is it Cindy?" I wondered if her answer was a result of the close relationship I thought we'd had or because I was so darn annoying as a first grader. Mrs. Warnecke told Chris Cuomo that "there was a connection back there" and continued by entertaining the studio audience with her quips: "I'm just glad this isn't a show about prisoners getting out and finding the teachers who ruined their lives."

There was a roar of laughter on the *Good Morning America* set, which made a nice contrast to all the tears that had been flowing only seconds before. I didn't notice until the show went to a commercial break and I was able to look around the studio, but there were tear-stained faces everywhere, in the audience, on the faces of the crew, and on my strapping former police detective/firefighter husband's cheeks.

After the segment, as we left to collect our things, people came spilling out of side rooms and offices—film editors and others—and they all wanted to tell me the same thing: "For me it was Mrs. McGillicutty in the third grade!" Everyone wanted to tell me their "Mrs. Warnecke" story.

Later that day, comments were posted on the *GMA* Web site:

> "So enjoyed the teacher story this morning. I just have one small request. Could you air the stories BEFORE 8:30 which is when I put on my makeup to go to work? I will have to either be late to work or have tear streaks running down my face all day."

> "The story about the woman who was inspired by her first grade teacher made me cry with utter joy. It still amazes me to hear stories like this of how one human being can change the life of another. This story was moving, inspiring, and beautiful. I was touched and honored to hear their story."

And now, months later, I have heard thousands of "Mrs. Warnecke" stories. Every time I tell my "teacher tale," or someone sees a video clip of that Back to School program, I hear stories of teachers. The words I said to Chris Cuomo are true: "Everyone has a Mrs. Warnecke. We all have these teachers who made a tremendous impact on our lives."

Not everyone is lucky enough to find that special teacher as I found mine. And as Mrs. Warnecke and I parted that day, each heading back to our homes, back to the same lives we had before September 5, 2008, I knew somehow that something had changed—that the woman who had changed my life in 1963 was about to make a difference again. I didn't know exactly how; I wasn't sure what her role would be in my life—we were, for the most part, strangers, tied together by a brief moment in time a

lifetime ago. But as I looked out the window of my plane bound
for North Carolina, I knew that I would never be the same, all
because—finally—I had found Mrs. Warnecke.

Mrs. Warnecke and I celebrate our reunion with Chris Cuomo, anchor for Good
Morning America. *Mrs. Warnecke is holding the copy of* You Read to Me,
I'll Read to You *that I brought her.*

"I think that it is terrific that with all of this, teachers are getting the publicity and recognition they deserve."

—B. WARNECKE, SEPTEMBER 18, 2008

EIGHT

Reflecting on the Meaning

The first thing I did once I arrived home from New York and my *Good Morning America* experience was to sit down and write Mrs. Warnecke a letter. Actually, I *typed* the letter instead of handwriting it, explaining in the opening of the letter that I had too much to say, too much to tell her, to handwrite it all.

We had spent only a brief amount of time together after our debut on national television—a quick breakfast just after the show ended, and then Dr. and Mrs. Warnecke had a plane to catch. (September, of course, is hurricane season, and several storms were on the move, so the Warneckes felt they needed to get back to Chicago as soon as possible.) But it was amazing how much information we shared in the brief amount of time that we sat together. Mrs. Warnecke worked on her omelet, and I was so excited I could barely eat my waffle while we reminisced about a school that both of us held in our memories.

Interestingly, it only took a couple of minutes for the teacher and child to become two teachers chatting with each other. It was so exciting for me to hear Mrs. Warnecke's version of the story—including how she felt when she first saw that basement classroom. She said she had just been offered the job, so she was both excited about the opportunity and extremely nervous thinking that the teaching experience she'd had previously—one year of high school history—would not help one bit. So when the door was opened and she saw the classroom for the first time, she felt, she told me, *relieved*. It would be isolated and private, she thought—away from the other classrooms—so she wouldn't be compared to other teachers. She went on to tell me that both she and the basement "were starting from scratch": her dark basement was a blank canvas that actually made her feel "I can do this."

She also described the day a few weeks later when President Kennedy was assassinated. Although I remember that day vaguely, especially that we were released early from school, Mrs. Warnecke's memories were more detailed and emotional. As a young voter in 1963, she held great respect for the president, and she remembered vividly the horror and sadness of the day. We were in the library that day, she told me, listening to the librarian read aloud, when another teacher came in to tell her what had happened. She remembered walking us back to the room immediately so that we could be dismissed from school. I could hear the sadness in her voice during the retelling, and I imagined being a young teacher and trying to contain my emotions while caring for a roomful of first graders. And I pictured myself as one of those first graders, sitting in the library listening to stories and then being confused as we were led down that long hallway and outside to our basement.

Mrs. Warnecke remembered other students from our class that year. I was able to tell her about them—how John, for example, had grown up to be our high school's quarterback and how Susan became a high school science teacher. We also talked about other staff members at Bragtown—the principal, the librarian, and various teachers we recalled. She did remember Mrs. Riley and shared the story of attending her funeral. As I listened to her account and pictured Mrs. Warnecke and her husband attending the funeral, I felt a shift of emotion. Mrs. Riley had not been just my teacher, briefly—she was someone's *family*, and I felt sad thinking of my *first* first-grade teacher. I also learned that after teaching school for several years, Mrs. Warnecke had become a talented photographer. I told her that I would like to see her work.

Before the Warneckes left for the airport, we exchanged phone numbers and addresses, but the time we'd had for reminiscing had been too brief. That's why I felt that I needed to write the letter: I wanted Mrs. Warnecke to understand some things that I hadn't had time to explain, about my first-grade insecurities, my dismay at being placed in a classroom with a teacher who was indifferent to me. But I began the letter with an apology:

Dear Mrs. Warnecke,

I decided to type this in the event I get too chatty and write myself right off the paper. I just want to thank you for flying to New York with tropical storms and hurricanes looming. I know your family must wonder about the crazy fifty-year-old woman who would summon you across the country. Please tell them that I'm not too crazy, but that

being a teacher . . . it was important to me that I let you
know that you made a difference.

A couple of days after I mailed the letter, I found a card from
Mrs. Warnecke in my mailbox. Affixed to the front of the card was
a photograph of two pink tulips. In the message, she referred to our
"whirlwind trip" to New York and said that it was more than she
"could process still." She thanked me for "validating" her life. I
couldn't believe that I would ever have been able to make a difference in the life of the very teacher who had changed mine!

Later, in an e-mail, Mrs. Warnecke told me that the two tulips
represented us—she'd chosen the image carefully for the first card
she sent me. More cards would come as the months went by, all
adorned with artistic photographs, and all meaningful and symbolic.

Coach Arbes and Mr. Rogers

There have been many teachers in my life who
made an impact on who I became in the professional
world. Parents, grandparents, and close friends aside, the two
most influential teachers were Coach Sam Arbes and Mr. Jay
Rogers.

Coach Sam Arbes taught geography. He taught with humor
and passion. We learned more than where country boundaries
or rivers were located. As we learned about different cultures,
he pushed us to think outside the box. He encouraged us to
become politically active; he had us work on campaigns and
share our own culture in our community. His example helped
ease some of the racial tensions in our school community.

I had the opportunity to express to him how much he influenced me to become a teacher. I was teaching at Cary High School and discovered he had retired to the community. I ran into him one day, and we were able to stay in touch for a short time before he passed away.

Jay Rogers, the National Teacher of the Year in 1972, had a huge impact on my life and on my decision to become an educator. He was an excellent teacher; what made him so effective was the fact that not only was he accomplished in the subject matter, he also understood high school students and their needs.

There was no time to be bored, no time was wasted, and if you were off task, you were in trouble. He held us accountable. He treated us as adults. He had very high expectations. He would argue with us (I now understand it was debate), and many times he made me mad or frustrated, because he pushed me to think differently and to challenge myself.

His intentions were to ensure we would be successful after high school. He encouraged us to be active in clubs and social organizations within the community. He made sure we had fun and at the same time learned more than just facts and dates.

I am now with the North Carolina Association of Educators. In 2005, NCAE honored all North Carolina teachers of the year. I was able to thank Mr. Rogers in front of his peers and a few of mine. It was a nice day to walk down Bulldog memory lane with him.

—Angela Farthing, Director, Center for Teaching and Learning, North Carolina Association of Educators

Passing Along the Gift

Since I have found Mrs. Warnecke, it has become more and more apparent to me how my first-grade experience shaped me years later as a teacher. I think back to that day when I watched Kenton draw his Orange People Pictures. As I leaned over him and spoke his name, it was almost as if I consciously thought, *What would Mrs. Warnecke do?* And I knew the answer. Mrs. Warnecke would accept Kenton for himself, the same way I did. Having this type of teaching modeled for me so early enabled me to become the same type of nurturing teacher. And in a way I have been able to "pay it forward" by providing the same sort of kindness to my students that was given to me in that first-grade classroom.

Kind, nurturing behavior is easy to practice with the lovable, teacher-pleasing students, but Mrs. Warnecke taught me that every child deserves that type of respect and affirmation.

This type of behavior is easy to practice with the lovable, teacher-pleasing students, but Mrs. Warnecke taught me that every child deserves that type of respect and affirmation—and that philosophy of teaching has been at the very core of who I have been as an educator for thirty years.

When I think of students who have needed me the most, who have needed me to take Mrs. Warnecke's gifts and pass them along, I think, of course, of Joey and that rubber room, but I also think of Mariann, another student I taught for a short time that same year. Mariann was already a troubled child by the time she arrived in seventh grade, and she would be in and out of my classroom as she spent much of the year trying to turn her life around in a school for troubled youth. When she was with me, though, I treated her with respect and concern.

Twice, Mariann wrote me long letters from that hospital school:

> I'm making A's and B's now. I wear clothes that fit, don't do drugs, or skip school. I have totally changed my attitude towards life, school, friends, family, my future, and my relationships. . . . That's all I really have to say except for the fact that you were my favorite teacher I ever had. I'm not playing around. You really were.

Sadly, years later I saw Mariann on the evening news, shackled and wearing an orange jumpsuit. She was charged with accessory to murder and was later convicted. Since then I have often asked myself if there was anything I could have done to change the path that her life took. As a veteran teacher looking back at my students—those who struggled as well as those who became successful—I can at least feel sure that I did "whatever it took" to be a caring teacher and to inspire all my students.

I make no claims to greatness. But as I look back over my career, I see many stories that defy odds and expectations. I continue to follow the lives of many of my students who live in my community, and some who began with a dismal outlook for the future have found their "happily ever after." Although I certainly don't take credit for those successes, I am satisfied knowing that I did everything I could during my brief time with them to ensure that they would grow to be happy, healthy citizens. It's an opportunity I take very seriously, the chance to make an impact as I stand in front of a classroom every day. And my understanding of how to make a difference with children had its roots in Mrs. Warnecke's classroom.

Recently, I was given the chance to tell my story across North Carolina as the state's Teacher of the Year—the story you've just read about an insecure first grader who becomes a struggling young teacher and finally learns how to be an educator who matters. After I tell my story to my audiences, I show them the video clip of my reunion with Mrs. Warnecke.* Then I say these words:

> Every time I show this clip, I hear the same story.
> Everyone has a Mrs. Warnecke. You, yourselves, are sitting
> there now thinking of your Mrs. Warnecke. We, as teachers,
> have the honor every day of being someone's Mrs.
> Warnecke.

And as I tell my story to educators, I tell them that I'd like to take it a step further and say that we have not only the honor but the responsibility, in fact the *obligation,* to be that teacher who makes a difference.

I have shared this story with thousands of teacher education majors, student teachers, and practicing classroom teachers. At the end of the presentation, people line up to tell me about their Mrs.

---

*The video clip can be viewed on the ABC News Web site at http://abcnews. go.com/gma/story?id=5726538&page=1.

Warnecke. Folks are eager to share their stories—the grade they were in when they had that special teacher and what that teacher did that was so important.

> *We have not only the honor but the responsibility, in fact the obligation, to be that teacher who makes a difference.*

Many times people in the audience tell me I have inspired them to teach or to stay in teaching—which is surprising to me when I think of the years that I needed inspiration myself! One Saturday after delivering my "Finding Mrs. Warnecke" presentation on a college campus, I was approached by a teacher as I was gathering my things to leave. It was a busy weekend, my granddaughter's birthday, and I had a list of errands to complete before the birthday party—including picking up my granddaughter's gift—so I was in a hurry. But when I turned around, I saw tears in the young woman's eyes.

"I'm struggling," she said. "I came here today unsure about my future as a teacher. You—and Mrs. Warnecke—have helped me understand why I do what I do. I'll be staying in the classroom. Thank you." At that point I realized that I have the opportunity not only to have a positive impact on my students but also to make a difference with teachers.

Not long after that day, I was asked to speak to a group of high school students a three-hour drive away. I had a previously scheduled meeting the night before the presentation, which meant that I would be traveling across the state, late at night, and staying in a hotel in an unfamiliar city. I also had a meeting the following afternoon, which would require me to hurry out of the morning presentation, hop in the car, and quickly drive back across the state.

Some other important things came up on that day—U.S. Senator Kay Hagan decided to visit me and tour my school, and my alma mater, the University of North Carolina at Chapel Hill, was playing for the national championship in basketball that night. It was going to be an extremely long couple of days, and I was disappointed not to be able to watch my team's run for the championship. I thought hard about cancelling the presentation, thinking that there was just too much going on that day . . . it was too far . . . I wouldn't be able to work it in . . .

Somehow I made it all work. I began the day early, met with the senator, jumped in the car to drive to a neighboring school district and do a presentation for new teachers, drove across town to speak at a Teacher of the Year dinner, and then listened to the basketball game on the radio as I drove late into the night on lonely country roads.

The next morning I delivered my message, said good-bye to my host, and hurried toward the entrance so that I could get to my next destination on time. As I reached to push open the door, a young man extended his hand to me.

"I want to tell you how much your presentation meant to me," said the tall African American high school senior. "I came here today because it meant missing school for a while and hanging with my friends. I had no idea your words would be life changing. I've made up my mind. I want to be a teacher."

Thinking about how close I had come to wriggling out of this particular presentation, I felt humbled by the honor, responsibility, and obligation I have to be a person who makes a difference to the teaching profession. And this, of course, is another way that the legacy of Barbara Warnecke can be paid forward.

Completing the Circle

Last semester, a university in North Carolina assigned a class of teacher education majors the task of going back and interviewing their own Mrs. Warneckes. Because those students are young, they most likely didn't have a difficult time finding their former teachers, but I love to think how the story of our reunion is propagating this way, like ripples from a flung pebble spreading on the surface of a pond.

I was excited to hear the other day that a board member in my school district was inspired to contact her Mrs. Warnecke after watching our reunion on television. It's a story that has been shared with me repeatedly—people who have seen my reunion story are now searching for their own special teachers. Glenda, a North Carolina teacher, sent me this message:

> For me it is Doloris Zborill, who taught my 10th grade
> English class and liked our one class so much that she
> insisted on teaching us 11th grade English the next year.
> She was a hoot! And a true believer in intellectual
> freedom.

The next day I received another message from Glenda:

> I searched for anyone named "Zborill," figuring it was an
> unusual enough name that anyone with it would be related

to my high school English teacher. And I found her
nephew!! He is going to put me in touch with her again!
Can you believe it?

Glenda's excitement is a testament to the importance of teachers
in all our lives.

Nashonda, a Special Needs teacher and friend with whom I
had the pleasure of teaching several years ago, wrote me
recently:

Did I tell you that your story has motivated me to find my
third grade teacher? She was a (white older) teacher at a
Catholic school who gave a little girl (who was Black and
poor and constantly reminded of it) her first Bible and the
ability to prove others wrong by believing in *myself*, not my
situation. I still have that Bible.

As teachers, finding our own Mrs. Warneckes out there and
letting them know about the impact they had—on our teaching
and on our lives in general—is a way to give back to those special
teachers. Mrs. Warnecke referred to this in an e-mail she sent me
shortly after our New York reunion. "I think someone would call
that a perfect circle," she wrote.

Recently I had the opportunity to hear Thomas M. Bloch,
former CEO of H&R Block, speak about his decision to leave the
corporate world and become a math teacher. One thing he said
particularly stuck with me: "When each of us does something to
repair the world, we repair a bit of ourselves." Whenever my story
touches a student or a teacher, I feel that I hold a small claim on
"repairing the world." And every time that happens, this former

little insecure first grader gains a bit of confidence and realizes the dream of being "the one" who makes a difference.

And although it sounds cliché (it can even be found cross-stitched on pillows; I have one that says "I touch the future. I teach"), there is no greater honor than making a difference in another human being's life. I am forever grateful to Mrs. Warnecke for showing me how.

❧ "Hopefully now we can fill each other in on the gaps and mundane items of our lives and continue what I hope is an ongoing connection that had a brief blip of forty years."

—B. WARNECKE, SEPTEMBER 17, 2008

Epilogue

I hadn't seen or heard from Mrs. Warnecke for over forty years when we were reunited in New York City in September 2008. I hadn't sat in her first-grade classroom since 1964, forty-four years before. But now I consider her a dear friend, and I can barely remember what it was like all those years when I didn't know where she was.

We exchange e-mails frequently and talk about our lives, our children, our grandchildren, and our aches and pains. We discuss sports—Mrs. Warnecke is a Cubs fan; I keep her up-to-date on my NFL Panthers and University of North Carolina Tarheels. She was the first person I called, after my mother and my children, to share the news that I had been selected as one of four finalists for National Teacher of the Year in 2009. She was excited beyond words, and we sat on the phone and gushed like two schoolgirls. Soon I received one of her photographs, a picture of a bright orange flower sitting amid some delicate white ones. The inscription read, "It's good to stand out in a crowd." Mrs. Warnecke is one enthusiastic cheerleader!

I continue to send her my poetry, a tradition that was started at Bragtown School decades ago, and she provides that much-anticipated feedback.

I was trembling with excitement when I opened a gift package from Mrs. Warnecke at Christmas. Inside were two ornaments—both ceramic pencils; one read "Mrs. Warnecke" and one read "Mrs. Teacher." Those were the first two ornaments I hung on my tree that year.

I am thrilled, just as I was as a child, when I see that familiar name on an envelope in my mailbox. I know the contents before I open the envelope: there will be a beautiful photograph that has been taken by my first-grade teacher, a picture that will hold a special meaning. Mrs. Warnecke's cards announce the seasons (I now have photographs of fall leaves and snowfalls) and document her visits to interesting places. My favorite is of a one-room school-house in the desert.

On the first card she wrote after our reunion—the one with the tulips—Mrs. Warnecke included these words: "Thank you for what you did, but most importantly, thank you for what you became."

To that I have to say thank *you,* Mrs. Warnecke, not for what I became but for what you helped make of me. Your molding and shaping of me during the earliest, most impressionable days of my life resulted in my becoming a teacher who will do whatever it takes to make a difference in the life of a child—just as you did for me in a dark basement classroom. That classroom is more than just a memory; it lives inside of me. I am forever grateful that I found you there.

EVERYONE HAS A MRS. WARNECKE

I hope you've enjoyed reading about the difference my first-grade teacher made in my life. Over the years as I've shared this story with my fellow teachers, pre-service educators, and friends, without fail they tell me of the Mrs. Warnecke in their own lives. Surely you have a teacher who made a difference for you—someone who accepted you for who you were, someone who challenged you to do better than you thought you were capable of, someone who inspired you. I would love to hear your stories. Please visit me at my blog, www.thedreamteacher.blogspot.com, and tell me about the teacher who made a difference for you!